The Next Greatest Generation

A Fatherly Conversation Between a Gen X Dad and the Men of Gen Z

Jeffrey Hogan, PhD

Table of Contents

Copyright

The Next Greatest Generation: *A Fatherly Conversation Between a Gen X Dad and the Men of Gen Z*

Published by Defiance Press & Publishing, LLC

Bulk orders of this book may be obtained by contacting Defiance Press & Publishing, LLC. www.defiancepress.com.

Defiance Press & Publishing, LLC

281-581-9300

publishing@defiancepress.com

Dedication

To my sons — Julian, Quinn, and Ian —

May you rise higher, live wiser, and love deeper than I ever did.
This book was written for you, and for every young man and woman who dares to become the next greatest generation.

Introduction: An Invitation to Greatness

"The only thing necessary for the triumph of evil is for good men to do nothing."
— **Edmund Burke**

The title of this book, *The Next Greatest Generation*, isn't a claim — it's a challenge. It's not saying that my generation, Generation X, has already achieved greatness, or that Generation Z has somehow fallen short. It's saying that greatness is still available — waiting for whoever has the courage, humility, and discipline to claim it.

The phrase "Greatest Generation" was originally given to the men and women who endured the Great Depression, fought and won World War II, and rebuilt a world out of ruin. They weren't called the greatest because they were perfect. They were called that because they answered when history called — because in a time of hardship and sacrifice, they chose duty over comfort, purpose over pleasure, and unity over division.

The truth is that every generation starts with that same potential. The challenge is whether it will be realized or wasted.

This book exists because I believe greatness is once again within reach — but it will require something radically different from the culture we've created. It will require character, courage, and conviction. It will require discipline in an age of distraction and purpose in a time when comfort is worshiped as the highest good.

And it will require a new kind of strength — not the brute strength of conquest, but the quiet strength of those who build, protect, and endure.

A Father's Purpose

I didn't set out to write a manifesto for an entire generation. I wrote this as a father — for my three sons — and for the generation they represent.

Every father hopes his children will surpass him. That's the natural order of things. The purpose of a generation is to hand off what it has learned — the wisdom earned through years of mistakes, struggles, and survival — so that the next can go further, faster, and wiser.

That's what this book is about: passing on what I've learned so that my sons — and your sons and daughters — can rise above the noise, confusion, and cynicism of our times and become the kind of men and women who rebuild what's been lost.

Gen X grew up in a world that was changing faster than anyone could keep up with. We were the bridge generation — analog childhoods, digital adulthoods. We learned independence not because it was fashionable, but because nobody was coming to rescue us. We were the latchkey kids, the first generation to see divorce as normal and self-reliance as survival.

We weren't perfect, but we were resilient. We learned how to adapt, how to fix things ourselves, and how to keep going even when the path wasn't clear.

That's the wisdom we need to pass on — not the nostalgia of the past, but the tools to survive the future.

The Generational Crossroads

Every generation faces a defining moment. For the Greatest Generation, it was global war. For the Baby Boomers, it was social revolution. For Gen X, it was economic uncertainty and the dawn of the digital age. For Gen Z, it's the overwhelming weight of information, the erosion of truth, and a world that feels increasingly disconnected and unstable.

The question isn't whether the challenges are real. They are. The question is what this generation will *do* with them.

Gen Z is the most connected generation in history — and paradoxically, one of the loneliest. They have access to more knowledge than any humans before them — and yet struggle to find meaning in it. They see the corruption and contradictions of our systems clearly — sometimes more clearly than we do — but they also wrestle with cynicism and fatigue before life has even begun.

That's why I believe the next great generation won't be defined by technology or politics or even wealth. It will be defined by *moral courage* — the courage to tell the truth when it's unpopular, to take responsibility when it's easier to blame, to serve others when the world says serve yourself.

These are not new virtues. They're ancient. But every generation has to rediscover them for itself.

Lessons from the Middle Generation

We, the Gen Xers, grew up between two extremes — the idealism of the Boomers and the digital speed of the Millennials. We learned how to adapt to both worlds, but also how to see through the illusions of each.

We learned that success without sacrifice is empty.
That comfort without purpose leads to despair.
That freedom without responsibility eventually collapses.

And we learned that wisdom doesn't come from certainty; it comes from struggle.

When I look at my sons' generation, I don't see weakness. I see potential — massive, untapped, world-changing potential. But I also see a generation that's being told lies: that truth is relative, that comfort equals happiness, and that life is about chasing experiences rather than building endurance.

This book is my attempt to cut through that noise. It's not about politics or culture wars. It's about character. It's about rediscovering the virtues that make people — and nations — strong.

The Power of Example

Every chapter that follows is built around a theme — resilience, failure, work ethic, money, relationships, freedom, and faith — but woven through them all is one simple truth: people don't rise to expectations; they rise to examples.

When I was your age, I didn't have social media, but I had mentors — men and women who showed me what strength looked like. Sometimes they taught through words, but more often through quiet consistency. They didn't need hashtags or applause. They just did what was right, day after day.

Today's generation is bombarded with information but starved for wisdom. The goal of this book is to offer that wisdom — not as a sermon, but as a conversation. A father talking to his sons about what it really takes to live well, love deeply, and leave something better behind.

Greatness Redefined

We often mistake greatness for fame, wealth, or recognition. But true greatness — the kind that lasts — comes from how you live when no one is watching.

It's found in discipline when no one is keeping score.
In honesty when lying would be easier.
In courage when fear whispers, "stay silent."

It's the same greatness that carried soldiers through frozen battlefields, that rebuilt nations from ashes, and that built families who stayed together when life got hard.

That kind of greatness is still possible — but it has to be chosen.

And that's what I want for my sons and their generation: to choose greatness not as a slogan, but as a way of life. To live as if their lives matter, because they do.

The Invitation

So, no — neither Gen X nor Gen Z is *yet* the greatest generation. But they could be — together.

Our generation has the wisdom of experience; theirs has the energy and innovation to transform it into something new. The handoff between generations is the most important exchange in human history. It's not about money or power or status. It's about values.

If we hand off bitterness, blame, and fear, we'll lose them. But if we hand off discipline, faith, and purpose, we'll give them something indestructible.

That's why this book exists. It's a letter from one generation to the next — a message from a Gen X dad to the sons who will inherit a world more complex than any before it yet filled with more opportunity than ever imagined.

The next greatest generation isn't defined by the year they were born. It's defined by the choices they make — the daily, quiet, uncompromising choices to live with honor, humility, and hope.

A Final Word to My Sons

To my sons — you've already made me proud. But my hope is that you never stop growing, never stop questioning, and never settle for less than the man you were made to be.

My generation made its share of mistakes. We chased comfort when we should have chased purpose. We traded attention for authenticity. But we've also learned — sometimes the hard way — that greatness isn't about avoiding pain; it's about transforming it into strength.

If you can learn that lesson sooner than I did, you'll already be ahead.

The world doesn't need another generation of victims. It needs a generation of builders — men and women who see through the fog, stand for truth, and rebuild what's been broken.

That's the kind of generation you were born to be.
That's what it means to become *The Next Greatest Generation.*

Chapter 1: Resilience in an Uncertain World

A deeper look at how resilience—shaped by setbacks, uncertainty, and persistence—becomes the foundation for growth, stability, and lasting success in a world that rarely plays fair.

Resilience is one of those words that doesn't come alive until you live through something that demands it. You can read about resilience in a book, nod at it during a motivational talk, or even hashtag it on social media. Still, you don't truly understand it until life knocks you off balance and you're forced to get back up.

For me, that day was September 11, 2001.

I remember the exact moment with absolute clarity. It was a little before 7:00 a.m. in Colorado Springs, and I was about to leave for work. My wife—eight months pregnant with our first son, Julian—was still asleep upstairs. I started my car, and the radio came alive with a news report about a fire in one of the World Trade Center towers. They speculated a small plane might have hit the building. It didn't sound real. Something inside me told me to go back inside and see it for myself.

I turned on CNN just in time for my wife to wake up and join me. Together we watched, stunned, as United Flight 175 slammed into the South Tower at 7:03 a.m. our time. The fireball erased any illusion of accident. At that moment, I knew our country was under attack.

I eventually drove into work, but I might as well not have. The office felt paralyzed. Colleagues gathered silently around the TV, staring at images that looked like they belonged in a Hollywood movie rather than the morning news. No one could concentrate, no one could work. I felt restless, anxious, powerless—like I had to *do* something. So, I went to the local blood bank to donate. I called my Air Force Reserve unit, secretly hoping to be mobilized, eager to contribute in some tangible way.

In the days and months that followed, I was called back to active duty, but not in the way I imagined. I wasn't shipped off to Afghanistan or Iraq like so many of my peers. Instead, I instructed space operators, training those who would deliver critical capabilities to warfighters across the globe. A month later, I watched my first son enter the world and wrestled with what kind of future he would inherit.

And here's where my struggle with resilience took on a different shape. Looking back, I didn't see myself as particularly heroic. I wasn't a soldier in combat. I wasn't on the front lines. I was in a safe location, teaching, supporting, and carrying out my duty as part of the rear guard. For years, I wrestled with the fact that my *"biggest contribution"* during the defining event of my lifetime didn't feel big enough. It didn't match the grand narrative of John Wayne storming the battlefield or Luke Skywalker taking on the Empire. My role was quieter, more ordinary.

But over time, I realized that resilience isn't always about having a Hollywood moment or about acts of bravery that make headlines. Most of the time, resilience is about enduring relentless uncertainty—showing up, day after day, and moving forward anyway.

That's why I believe resilience is the most essential skill of our time. For my generation, Gen X, resilience was forged in childhoods shaped by divorce and economic instability, in careers built through recessions and layoffs, in lessons learned the hard way when the dot-com bubble burst. For your generation, Gen Z, resilience is being tested in different ways: a pandemic that rewrote the rules of daily life, climate anxiety, the rapid pace of technological disruption, and the weight of social media amplifying every crisis in real time.

The situations are different, but the principle is the same. Resilience isn't a trait some people are born with. It's a set of skills, habits, and mindsets earned through hardship. It doesn't come from comfort—it comes from facing adversity and learning not just to bounce back, but to adapt, grow, and keep going.

That's what this chapter is about. First, I'll share how Gen X was shaped by our own constant stream of uncertainty. Then, we'll compare how resilience plays out differently for Gen Z. I'll lay out practical advice to help you strengthen this essential skill. Finally, I'll leave you with a challenge to apply resilience in your own life this month.

Because if there's one thing I've learned, it's this: *every generation is tested by the storms of its time.* What defines you is how you respond.

When people describe Gen X, they often reach for labels: the "latchkey kids," the "forgotten middle child" between Boomers and Millennials, the "slackers" of the early '90s. But behind the stereotypes lies something deeper—resilience built from uncertainty, often starting in childhood.

For me, that uncertainty started at age eight, when my parents divorced. Within a year, my mom remarried, and our family uprooted from the California Bay Area to rural Oklahoma. Overnight, my world shifted from suburban comfort to a 5-acre patch of tick-infested land where we lived out of a tent while my stepdad built a metal shop for his water pump business. It took two years before we lived in a real house. That was resilience lesson number one: **sometimes life strips things down to the essentials, and you adapt because you have no choice.**

By sixteen, I was determined to earn my own money. In Tahlequah—a town of about 10,000 at the time—getting hired wasn't easy if you weren't connected to the family who owned the business. After being turned down at half a dozen places, I finally landed a job at the new Hardee's restaurant. Minimum wage was $3.35 an hour, and even that felt like a gift. With every paycheck, I gained a little independence and the confidence that I could stand on my own two feet.

Then, at seventeen, that independence evolved into outright rebellion: a falling out with my mom sent me back to California to live with my dad and stepmom. Suddenly, I was back in the heart of Silicon Valley. If Tahlequah had taught me the value of scraping by, Los Altos showed me a new kind of pressure.

My new school—Homestead High—was the alma mater of Apple co-founder Steve Wozniak. At lunch, I'd hear classmates talk casually about their parents' stock options or internships in the booming tech industry. Some of my peers had allowances larger than I made working part-time at McDonald's. One friend even got caught breaking into the computer lab at Stanford, where our school kept its grade records—not because he had to, but to prove he could. The school suspended him, but Hewlett-Packard hired him for $23,000 a year the next day. For a sixteen-year-old in 1984, that was a fortune. These were the life lessons I was now learning: *that breaking rules sometimes led to opportunity in Silicon Valley.*

The culture shock was intense. Where I had once been grateful to get a job, now I was surrounded by people who treated opportunity as an entitlement. And just as I adjusted, the news broke that students at my school were cheating on the SAT—paying others to take the test. Think about that: *how smart do you have to be to guarantee someone else a score high enough to get into a top college?* These weren't ordinary criminals; they were bored adolescents, often smarter than the Boomer teachers overseeing them. The pressure to perform academically wasn't just high—it was cutthroat.

I chose a different path. Influenced by the values I'd picked up in Oklahoma—hard work, independence, a respect for service—I set my sights on the Air Force. Oklahoma State offered me a strong engineering program and an ROTC path to becoming an officer. Plus, OSU put me back into an environment I understood and respected—unlike the Bay Area, which seemed to operate on the unspoken rule that it was only wrong if you got caught. For the first couple of years, I thrived. I even made the Dean's List my freshman year. But then came resilience lesson number two: **sometimes the most brutal battles are the ones you fight with yourself.**

My bad study habits began to catch up to me. I skipped classes when I felt like sleeping in. I crammed for exams at the last minute. And when money got tight, I often chose work over study time. I took out student loans, picked up jobs to make ends meet, and slowly watched my academic confidence erode. Eventually, I transferred back to California to finish at San Jose State, limping across the finish line with a physics degree and a GPA that barely kept me afloat.

On paper, that sounds like failure. But here's the thing about resilience: *it doesn't always look pretty.* Sometimes resilience is surviving your own mistakes. Sometimes it's stumbling forward, paying off debt one dollar at a time, and learning the hard way that shortcuts in life usually cost more in the end.

When I was commissioned as an Air Force officer and earned a measly $1,387 a month, I understood two things deeply: one, that money could disappear faster than you earned it, and two, that no one would hand me stability. Resilience wasn't about being fearless but about staying in the game when everything in you wanted to quit.

That was the Gen X reality. We weren't all coddled—at least not most of us. Participation trophies hadn't yet become a thing. We weren't always celebrated, and we weren't handed a roadmap. Instead, we learned to figure things out on our own, to adapt to shifting environments, and to survive uncertainty with a mix of stubbornness and independence.

But uncertainty wasn't just personal but economic, cultural, and technological. And nowhere was that more evident than in the Dot-Com Bubble.

I graduated from Homestead High School in Cupertino in 1985, right in the heart of Silicon Valley. A decade later, many people I'd grown up with were chasing the internet gold rush. Between 1995 and 2000, the NASDAQ rose by 400%, driven almost entirely by internet-based companies. In 1999 alone, there were 457 IPOs, with 117 doubling in price on their first day of trading. Startups with no revenue were suddenly valued in the hundreds of millions—sometimes billions—based on a catchy name ending in ".com."

For a moment, it felt like the rules had changed. Friends and classmates left steady jobs to become day traders. Others joined startups, lured by stock options that promised instant wealth. People bought into the idea that you couldn't lose. But then came March of 2000, when the NASDAQ peaked at 5,048. By October 2002, it had plummeted to 1,139—wiping out nearly 80% of its value. Five trillion dollars in market value evaporated, and more than half of all dot-com startups disappeared almost overnight.

For Gen X, many of us in our twenties and early thirties at the time, this was resilience lesson number three: **if something seems too good to be true, it probably is.** The dream of being a millionaire by 25 quickly turned into the reality of being broke by 26.

The experience left its mark. It made us skeptical of promises of overnight success and cautious with our money. It has also shaped how we respond to the new financial fads that tempt today's younger generations—cryptocurrency, NFTs, and digital speculation. When Gen X shrugs and says, "*We've seen this movie before,*" it isn't cynicism for its own sake—

it's the memory of real paychecks, real savings, and real futures that vanished in a crash.

But resilience is about more than just avoiding mistakes. It's about adapting after you've been burned. Many of my peers returned to traditional careers, more grounded and disciplined than before. Others doubled down, building the companies that endured—Amazon, eBay, Google, PayPal. Gen X carried the lessons of the dotcom bust forward, not as a cautionary tale alone, but as a reminder that resilience means taking the hit, absorbing the lesson, and moving forward wiser.

The Dot-Com bust taught us hard financial lessons, but in truth, Gen X was already prepared for disappointment. Long before the bubble burst, the media branded us the *"doomed generation."*

In the late '80s and early '90s, magazine covers, and news broadcasts made it clear that Gen X would be the first generation to do worse than our parents. *Time Magazine* famously ran a 1990 cover calling us "Lazy, Cynical, and Disaffected." [1] We were labeled slackers who lacked ambition, a generation of underachievers destined to drift.

That narrative seeped into how we saw ourselves, and it was hard to escape. At the same time, we were fighting through economic realities that reinforced the idea: stagnant wages, rising student debt, and two recessions before many of us hit our 30s[2]. Yet, despite the predictions, Gen X adapted, endured, and eventually found stability.

Today, Gen Z faces a similar mix of challenges and stigma. But while the struggles overlap, the tools and culture shaping your generation differ. Let's break down the parallels and contrasts.

Economic Struggles

Gen X entered the workforce during two recessions (early 1990s and 2001) [3]. Many of us had to shoulder student debt without significant parental support. Housing, like today's

Gen Z situation, felt out of reach. Boomers outnumbered us and held onto jobs and homes longer, creating bottlenecks. By age 30, about 48% of Gen X owned homes. That was lower than that of Boomers (51%) but still far higher than today's Millennials (42%)[4]. We heard endlessly that we'd "never own homes" or "never retire," yet many of us eventually did both.

In contrast, Gen Z entered the workforce during the COVID-19 pandemic and its economic fallout. They face record student debt, inflation, and a housing market where starter homes are scarce and unaffordable[5]. Gig economy jobs and contract work dominate, creating instability but also flexibility.

Parallel: Both generations launched careers in economies stacked against them. Both were told they'd be the first generation to do worse than their parents.

Technology Shaping Resilience

Gen X saw technology shaping its resilience. We grew up analog. If you wanted a song, you made a mixtape—waiting by the radio to press record. We endured dial-up internet and the screech of modems, where getting online meant waiting. Technology taught patience. It demanded workarounds[6]. During the Dot-Com era, we saw firsthand how tech could create—or destroy—fortunes overnight. That skepticism still lingers in how we approach financial and career risks.

Gen Z, by comparison, is a digital native generation. Smartphones, streaming, and instant access to information have always been the baseline[7]. The upside is incredible access to knowledge, global connection, and opportunity. The downside is relentless exposure to crises, global comparisons, and the pressure to perform at internet speed.

Parallel: Both generations had technology redefine their worlds. Gen X had to learn patience and adaptability, while Gen Z learned discernment and mental discipline in a world of constant information.

Stigma from Older Generations

Gen X was branded as slackers, cynical, and disaffected. Boomers accused us of lacking a work ethic. We were told we'd never achieve what they did—yet we eventually surpassed them in median income and built many of the tech foundations the world relies on today[8].

Gen Z has received its own labels: "fragile," "overly online," and "entitled." Older generations mock safe spaces and cancel culture as signs of weakness[9]. Yet, Gen Z has shown a willingness to confront issues head-on—climate change, social justice, and mental health—in ways previous generations avoided[10].

Parallel: Both generations have been underestimated and dismissed by those before them. Both have responded by building resilience in ways that defy stereotypes.

How Resilience Is Shaped

A pattern begins to emerge between Gen X and Gen Z in how each shapes its own form of resilience.

For Gen X, resilience grew out of independence and skepticism. We didn't have GoFundMe, TikTok support groups, or wellness apps. If something broke, we fixed it. If money ran short, we picked up another job. If we got laid off, we hustled for the next opportunity. The "latchkey" childhood meant learning to handle life alone early. Feeding ourselves after school, managing schedules, and dealing with boredom without constant entertainment made us resourceful[11].

For Gen Z, resilience grows out of digital community and activism. When crisis hits, Gen Z leans on networks—sometimes virtual, sometimes real—to problem-solve and push for change. The ability to mobilize quickly, raise awareness, and harness digital tools is a new form of resilience[12].

Parallel: Where Gen X resilience came from self-reliance, Gen Z resilience often comes from collective action. Both are valid; both reflect the environment each generation grew up in.

Mental Health and Pressure

For Gen X, mental health wasn't openly discussed. Anxiety, depression, and burnout existed, but they weren't acknowledged. You pushed through, often alone. The result was toughness, yes, but also scars[13].

For Gen Z, mental health is front and center. Gen Z has normalized therapy, medication, and conversations about anxiety and depression[14]. The result is awareness, openness, and the weight of constant self-diagnosis and the pressure of being "always on." [15]

Parallel: Both generations wrestle with mental health in their own way. Gen X learned to suppress; Gen Z learned to confront. Resilience requires a balance of strength and self-awareness.

In the end, the similarities matter more than the differences. And it shouldn't be overlooked that Gen Z are, quite literally, the children of Gen X. Many of the lessons my generation learned about resilience were intended to be passed down. If there is one clear sign of progress, Gen Z's openness to mental health may be one of the most positive outcomes of that inheritance.

Gen X was told we were doomed; Gen Z hears the same. We fought through instability, adapted to technology, bore the weight of stigma, and developed resilience along the way. So will you.

Everyone agrees that resilience is essential, but few people explain *how* to build it. It's not a magic trait. It's a set of choices, habits, and perspectives that add up over time. Those lessons came the hard way for Gen X—through recessions, layoffs, failed ventures, and life's everyday curveballs. The question is: *what can Gen Z take from those experiences to build their own foundation of resilience?*

Adaptability as Survival

The first lesson is adaptability. Gen X entered a workforce that looked stable on paper but constantly shifted underneath. Companies downsized, jobs evaporated, and entire industries reshaped themselves. We became masters at pivoting—learning new skills, freelancing, and taking side hustles long before it was fashionable.

After leaving active duty in the Air Force and moving into contracting, I began mentoring younger military members preparing to transition into the private sector. Many believed the stories that contracting jobs would be waiting with huge pay raises as soon as they left the military. I had to give them a reality check. I told them, “You’re giving six months’ notice when you leave. But contractors hire for immediate needs. They aren’t waiting around for you.” My advice was simple: *take whatever job is offered when you leave.* Don’t get picky. Don’t chase the myth of instant big money. Prove yourself, gain two years of experience, and then use that credibility to move into a better role.

That advice came straight from my generation’s experience: *adaptability isn’t glamorous.* Sometimes, resilience means humbling yourself, taking the less-than-ideal first step, and trusting that persistence will open bigger doors down the road.

The Power of Mental Toughness

The second lesson is toughness—not the movie version, but the everyday kind. Gen X learned that life throws constant setbacks, and sometimes, you simply must push through. We didn’t always talk about it, but the truth is, grit and perseverance were often the only tools we had.

Resilience doesn't mean never failing. It means refusing to let failure define you. That bad grade, that layoff, that startup collapse—they don't have to be the headline of your life. Whether you pick yourself up, adjust, and keep moving forward matters.

Self-Reliance with Smart Networking

The third lesson is a balance between independence and connection. Gen X grew up with self-reliance drilled into us —we fixed things ourselves, budgeted carefully, and didn't expect institutions to bail us out. That independence-built strength, but it also risked isolation.

Gen Z, by contrast, has mastered the art of leveraging networks—whether through online communities, activism, or collective problem-solving. The smartest path forward combines both. Build your personal skills so you never depend entirely on others but also cultivate a trusted circle that can help you through the crises no one can handle alone.

The Discipline of Delayed Gratification

Finally, there's the lesson that may be the hardest to embrace in a world of instant everything: *delayed gratification*. Gen X learned it through necessity. The Dot-Com crash reminded us that shortcuts don't last, and the 2008 financial crisis reminded us again. Resilience means having the patience to play the long game.

I often told people transitioning out of the military that job-hopping could be useful, but only if used sparingly. Jump too quickly and you burn your credibility. Stick it out long enough, build up your track record, and then cash in that credibility for something better. In other words, resilience is about resisting the urge for instant payoff and learning when to wait.

I also saw this lesson firsthand as a hiring manager. Suppose I see a resume with four jobs in six years. In that case, it usually doesn't even get a second look—it doesn't matter how talented or qualified the person is. What's worse is watching people broadcast their frustrations on LinkedIn, complaining about setbacks or bad companies. Air your laundry at the bar or over dinner with friends—not in front of the people who may one day decide whether to hire you. Ignore the "likes" and positive comments those posts get; those people won't be signing your paycheck. Someone like me will.

What do I look for? The right balance of experience and someone who has done their time. During interviews, I always sneak in questions about adversity. About seven years ago, I interviewed a young woman named Shannon, a Millennial, for an entry-level analyst role. She had a personal recommendation from a trusted coworker, but I was cautious. She performed well in the interview, but what struck me most came at the end when I asked if she had any questions. She asked how long it would take before benefits kicked in. She explained that she was a single mom with an eight-year-old son and needed to plan how to cover his medical insurance during the gap. That question told me everything I needed about her maturity, priorities, and work ethic.

Today, Shannon still works in the company—loyal, hardworking, and thriving. She's married to a great husband and father, has a second child, a house, and a master's degree in business. She has become an up-and-coming leader in the organization and one of the best hiring decisions I have ever made. Her story proves that resilience, delayed gratification, and persistence build careers and lives.

Think of it like compound interest: small deposits of effort, patience, and persistence add up over time. The flashy overnight success stories usually flame out. The people who endure, who save their wins for the right opportunities, are the ones who build lasting success.

Resilience, then, isn't abstract. It's practical. It's adaptability, toughness, independence, balanced with connection, and the discipline to delay gratification. Anyone can develop these tools—if you're willing to practice them.

Here's a reality check...Getting discouraged during the struggle is common, but resilience pays off in the long run. For all the predictions that Gen X would never own homes or achieve financial stability, we eventually did. By age 30, nearly half of us had become homeowners—lower than Boomers but still well ahead of Millennials. Gen X households earn more than any other generation today, with median household income reaching approximately $101,500 in 2022, the highest across all age groups[16].

The lesson? Resilience doesn't always deliver quick wins, but it creates steady progress with time, persistence, adaptability, and grit that compound into real, lasting success.

Resilience isn't glamorous. It doesn't often make headlines or viral posts. But the quiet, steady force that carries you through uncertainty and eventually shapes success. Gen X learned this through years of setbacks and slow progress; the results speak for themselves. Despite being branded the *"doomed generation,"* we found ways to adapt, survive, and eventually thrive.

Gen Z now faces its own set of storms—pandemics, housing crises, inflation, climate anxiety, and the relentless noise of the digital age. The temptation is to believe the headlines, to let the weight of negativity convince you that your future is already written. But here's the truth: *resilience rewrites the story.*

Every generation is tested. Every generation hears some version of *"you won't make it."* And every generation that rises above does so because ordinary people choose persistence over despair, effort over excuses, growth over giving up.

So, here's my challenge: **identify one area in your life this month where you will deliberately practice resilience.** It could be sticking to a budget, pushing through a challenging fitness goal, finishing a project you've been tempted to abandon, or simply handling a failure with grace instead of frustration. Make it small, make it concrete, but commit to it.

Resilience isn't built in a single dramatic moment—it's forged in the everyday decisions to keep going when quitting would be easier.

Gen X was told we were doomed, and we proved otherwise. Now it's your turn. The Next Greatest Generation won't be defined by how easy the world makes things for you, but by how you rise when the world makes things hard. If I were to sum up the concept of resilience, it would be this: **it's not about bouncing back—it's about refusing to stay down.** And from where I stand, you already have everything it takes.

---

[1] *Time Magazine*, July 16, 1990. Cover story labeling Gen X as "Lazy, Cynical, and Disaffected."

[2] Bureau of Labor Statistics (BLS). *Labor Force Statistics from the Current Population Survey.* Gen X entered workforce during recessions in 1990–91 and 2001; Gen Z entered during the COVID-19 downturn in 2020.

[3] Bureau of Labor Statistics (BLS). *Labor Force Statistics from the Current Population Survey.* Gen X entered workforce during recessions in 1990–91 and 2001; Gen Z entered during the COVID-19 downturn in 2020.

[4] U.S. Census Bureau. *Current Population Survey, Housing Vacancy Survey, 1980–2018.* Data shows homeownership rates by age and generation (Gen X ~48% at age 30, Boomers ~51%, Millennials ~42%)

[5] Pew Research Center. (2014). *The Generations Defined.* Gen X as the first generation to adopt digital tech but raised analog (rotary phones, mixtapes, dial-up).

[6] Pew Research Center. (2014). *The Generations Defined.* Gen X as the first generation to adopt digital tech but raised analog (rotary phones, mixtapes, dial-up).

[7] Pew Research Center. (2019). *Defining Generations: Where Millennials End and Generation Z Begins*. Clarifies Gen Z as "digital natives."

[8] Howe, N., & Strauss, W. (1993). *13th Gen: Abort, Retry, Ignore, Fail?* Classic work on Gen X independence and skepticism.

[9] Twenge, J. M. (2006). *Generation Me*. Outlines perceptions of entitlement and fragility among Millennials/ Gen Z by older generations.

[10] Parker, K., & Igielnik, R. (2020). *On the Cusp of Adulthood and Facing an Uncertain Future: What We Know About Gen Z So Far.* Pew Research Center. Highlights stigma and economic challenges facing Gen Z.

[11] Pew Research Center. (2014). *Millennials in Adulthood.* Notes latchkey Gen X independence vs. collectivism among younger generations.

[12] Twenge, J. M. (2017). *iGen: Why Today's Super-Connected Kids Are Growing Up Less Rebellious, More Tolerant, Less Happy—and Completely Unprepared for Adulthood.* Documents Gen Z's openness about mental health compared to Gen X's silence.

[13] Howe, N., & Strauss, W. (1993). *13th Gen: Abort, Retry, Ignore, Fail?* Classic work on Gen X independence and skepticism.

[14] American Psychological Association (2019). *Stress in America: Generation Z.* Shows Gen Z reports the highest levels of stress and is most open about mental health.

[15] Twenge, J. M. (2017). *iGen: Why Today's Super-Connected Kids Are Growing Up Less Rebellious, More Tolerant, Less Happy—and Completely Unprepared for Adulthood.* Documents Gen Z's openness about mental health compared to Gen X's silence.

[16] *Erin Bendig, Median Income by Generation: How Do You Compare? Kiplinger Magazine, updated 11 February 2025*

Chapter 2: The Myth of Overnight Success

A reality check on hustle culture, success timelines, and the importance of patience, adaptability, and sustained effort in career and life.

Did you know the average startup takes seven to ten years to achieve real success—if it survives that long? According to the Harvard Business Review[1], nearly two-thirds of startups never deliver a positive return to their investors. Yet when we scroll through social media, binge on business podcasts, or hear viral success stories, we believe that fame, fortune, and career breakthroughs can happen almost instantly.

This is the myth of overnight success—the belief that greatness happens in a flash. It's an illusion that hustle culture thrives on, selling the fantasy that if you just grind harder and longer, your big break will be right around the corner. For Gen Z, growing up in a world where algorithms can make someone famous overnight, this tale is especially seductive—and dangerous. Because while going viral might happen in a day, building something that lasts takes patience, adaptability, and years of effort.

Gen X knows this story all too well, even though the setting was different. I remember growing up in the middle of Silicon Valley in the late '90s when the dot-com boom had everyone chasing internet gold. Friends of mine quit stable jobs to join flashy startups that promised stock options worth millions. They imagined early retirement, luxury cars, and beachfront homes. But, when the bubble burst in 2000 and 2001, most of those companies evaporated almost overnight[2]. My friends didn't end up wealthy—they ended up back at square one, with resumes that had more gaps than growth. The "*overnight success*" they were promised turned out to be a mirage.

Fast forward to today, and the stage has shifted from boardrooms to smartphones. A 19-year-old can post a TikTok dance and gain a million followers in a week[3]. Brand deals start rolling in, money starts flowing, and it feels like success has arrived. But just as quickly, the audience moves on. Engagement plummets, deals dry up, and the influencer faces the crushing reality that they built a career on shifting sand. Some reinvent themselves, but many burn out, left with nothing more than a spike of fleeting fame.

Both stories—Gen X and Gen Z—show the same truth. Overnight success is rarely what it seems. The same lesson applies to whether you were chasing dot-com millions or viral fame: *What looks instant is usually years in the making, and what fades fast is rarely sustainable.*

In this chapter, I'll unpack why the myth of overnight success persists, how hustle culture distorts expectations, and what Gen Z can learn from Gen X's long, winding road. I'll explore the similarities and differences between the two generations, share lessons that stand the test of time, and ultimately show why patience, adaptability, and steady effort matter more than instant wins.

Because if Gen Z truly is the "*Next Greatest Generation,*" it won't be because of one viral moment. It will be because they commit to building something that lasts.

Growing up Gen X, you learn early that nothing is guaranteed and nothing comes fast. For my generation, Gen X, there was no such thing as overnight success. In fact, if you thought you were on the fast track, chances are reality was waiting to teach you a hard lesson. My own career was shaped by that reality.

I started my career in the Air Force right after the Cold War. On paper, it was supposed to be a time of opportunity—we had won the great race against the Soviets, and America was adjusting to its *"peace dividend."* But inside the service, it looked very different. The military was shrinking. Budgets were tight. Promotions were slow. And something called a RIF—a reduction in force—emerged from seemingly nowhere and hung over our heads like a storm cloud.

The term RIF sounds bureaucratic, but the impact was devastating. A RIF meant that even good officers, the kind of people you looked up to, could be cut loose simply because the Air Force no longer had room for them. I had friends and mentors who were shown the door, not because they lacked talent, but because the numbers didn't work out. The message was clear: *nothing was guaranteed.* Not even the sacred 20-year retirement we all thought was our baseline. It was a stark reminder that security could vanish overnight.

And my own journey? It wasn't a straight line either. I had joined with my eyes set firmly on space operations—a field that felt exciting, meaningful, and on the cutting edge of national defense. But the Air Force had other plans. I was reassigned to the missile career field, a path that, at the time, was considered about as undesirable as it got. It felt like being moved off the field just as the game got good. Nothing was fair about being pulled out of the arena I'd trained for and placed on the sidelines.

When I eventually left active duty, in disgust, I thought contracting would give me more control over my career. For a while, it worked. I found my place, built relationships, and gained new experiences. Then came another reality check. The company failed to win enough new contracts, and I was laid off just like that. It didn't matter that my record shouted out exceptional performer. One day, I had a future; the next, I wondered how I would pay bills for my wife and three school-aged kids.

Eventually, I swallowed my pride and took a one-person analyst job. It felt like surrender. It was lonely, small, and not the kind of position you brag about at reunions. But I showed up, did the work, and treated it as if it mattered. And over time, something incredible happened. That role grew. It expanded, slowly at first, adding two positions to keep up with demand, then five, then more rapidly. Ten years later, what had started as a desk for one person had become an operation of over a hundred people under my management.

It taught me something that would stay with me: *embrace the suck.* Those difficult years, the setbacks, the jobs that felt beneath me—they weren't wasted. They were the very experiences that forced me to develop critical skills, resilience, and expertise. In hindsight, they made me a better leader and manager. What doesn't kill us can make us stronger if we're willing to learn from it.

Gen X was shaped by challenges that came at us on every level—personal, institutional, and even national. On the personal side, losing my contracting job when the company failed to bring in enough business was a direct blow. It wasn't abstract—it was my livelihood, my family's security, gone overnight. On the institutional side, the Air Force RIF was a reminder that even a career in uniform, something you thought was steady, could be cut short by forces outside your control. And then there were national challenges, like the 2008 financial crash, which rippled far beyond Gen X. It wiped out retirement savings, killed jobs, and reshaped entire industries—not just for us, but for Millennials starting out and even Boomers trying to retire. Each type of challenge demanded something different from us—adaptability at the personal level, endurance at the institutional level, and resilience at the national level. Taken together, they taught us that setbacks come in many forms, and that surviving them makes you stronger in ways no shortcut to success ever could.

We also built careers before the digital age made networking instantaneous. There was no LinkedIn to connect you to a hiring manager in seconds, and no algorithm to make your résumé viral. If you wanted to move up, you went back to school, got the degree, built experience brick by brick, and networked in person. Success came, if at all, slowly.

That's the Gen X perspective: *success is long, messy, and unpredictable*. And yet, that's precisely why it lasts.

Now, let's fast forward to Gen Z, because the surface of the story looks completely different. Take Jimmy Donaldson, better known as MrBeast. Today, he's one of the most successful YouTubers in the world. Billions of views. Sponsorships. Businesses. If you stumbled on him now, you'd think his rise was meteoric, that he just figured out the secret formula and instantly became famous. But peel back the layers and you find a very different story.

MrBeast started uploading videos at 13[4]. For years, almost nobody watched. His content wasn't polished. His experiments didn't always work. He spent hundreds of hours learning how YouTube's algorithm worked, teaching himself editing tricks, and figuring out what people wanted to watch. He even did bizarre endurance stunts—like counting to 100,000 on camera—just to push the limits of attention. It wasn't glamorous. It wasn't fun. It was years of grinding, failing, and trying again. Only after all that invisible effort did his so-called *"overnight success"* finally arrive.

From the outside, Gen X and Gen Z look worlds apart. But the truth is the same. Whether you're an officer trying to navigate a downsizing military, a contractor laid off after a business loss, or a teenager uploading videos into the void, success doesn't come in a flash. It comes after years of patience, pivots, and persistence.

And that's the perspective I want to share with Gen Z. You may feel pressure to "make it" by 20, 25, or even earlier. But the truth is, the things that last—the careers, the reputations, the legacies—are built over time. And if you can learn to embrace that long game, you'll be stronger for it.

Gen X and Gen Z grew up hearing a simple mantra: "*Work hard and you'll succeed.*" It's part of the American dream—and for decades, it's been a central pillar of defining success. Yet today, that narrative is unraveling. According to a 2025 Wall Street Journal–NORC poll[5], only 25% of Americans believe they have a good chance of improving their standard of living, marking the lowest confidence level since records began in 1987. Nearly 70% say that the belief that hard work guarantees upward mobility no longer holds true—or never did.

That pessimism is particularly striking and hauntingly familiar to someone like me. My generation entered the workforce in the mid-'80s, when global events and shifting job markets made opportunity feel scarce. This shows that disillusionment isn't a generational fluke—it persists whenever reality outpaces the cultural narrative. Both generations have grappled with that tension: *being told effort is the key to success, then facing discouraging evidence to the contrary.*

Beyond the sentiment, Gen X and Gen Z have encountered the sting of expectations colliding with reality. Whether it was a startup that never took off, a viral post that fell flat, or a dream job that slipped away, both generations have learned the same hard lesson: *"work hard" doesn't always mean "get far."*

The most significant contrast between Gen X and Gen Z comes down to the speed of feedback and the perception of shortcuts. Gen Z has grown up in a world of instant validation—likes, shares, retweets, follower counts. Viral fame can feel attainable within hours. That immediacy distorts expectations: *"If I don't hit 10,000 likes fast, what's the point?"* In that environment, impatience thrives, and visibility itself can start to feel like the measure of value.

Gen X, on the other hand, learned the long game. Opportunities came through networking events, degree programs, mentorship, and years of consistent effort.

Feedback loops were slow—not instant, not viral—and while that demanded patience, it made success feel more substantial and anchored.

Think of the chase for a *"big break."*

Take a cultural icon of my generation: *Kurt Cobain and the grunge band Nirvana*. To the world, they seemed to burst onto the scene in 1991. But behind that apparent explosion were years of grinding—playing to tiny crowds in dingy clubs, sleeping in vans, refining their sound, and building a following that no one saw coming. Their rise wasn't sudden; it was the long, invisible labor finally breaking into view.

And it wasn't just Nirvana. Decades earlier, the Beatles had the same story. Before they became household names, they spent years in Hamburg, playing thousands of hours to half-interested bar crowds. They were already seasoned performers when they landed on *The Ed Sullivan Show*. What looked like an overnight phenomenon was the payoff of relentless practice and persistence.

Today's parallels are found on TikTok, YouTube, and other digital platforms. Consider Noah Beck[6], a male Gen Z creator who rocketed to stardom with tens of millions of followers. He looked like he had *"made it"* instantly to the outside world. But Beck has spoken openly about the reality: *sudden visibility brought overwhelming pressure, anxiety, unrealistic expectations, and the constant fear that his fame could vanish as quickly as it came*. His story shows the seductive speed of modern success—and the hidden fragility beneath it.

When we compare Gen X and Gen Z, a clear narrative emerges. Both generations were sold on the promise that hard work would guarantee success, and both discovered how hard it is to live up to that expectation.

Gen X, over time, learned to endure slow, laborious progress. Gen Z, in contrast, will continue to wrestle with instant visibility and volatile validation. Classic dreamers and today's digital natives may walk different paths, but both walk uphill—and it is in that uphill climb that strength is built. Whether playing to empty rooms, grinding in cubicles for years, or chasing Likes that disappear overnight, the core lesson holds true: *lasting success isn't fast, but it is real.*

If there's one lesson that bridges the gap between generations, it's this: *success is a long game.* The myth of the shortcut—the overnight break, the viral post, the one big moment—is precisely that: *a myth.* What really matters is persistence, process, and patience.

If I were to summarize my practical life lessons when it comes to dealing with the illusion of overnight success, I would recommend the following:

First, redefine success as something measured in years, not weeks. Great careers, lasting businesses, and meaningful lives aren't built on flashes but foundations.

Second, focus on the process, not just the outcome. The process is where skills develop, resilience is formed, and adaptability is tested. Success that lasts comes from who you become along the way, not just what you achieve at the end.

Third, set realistic timelines. In *Outliers*, Malcolm Gladwell popularized the idea that mastery often takes 10,000 hours of deliberate practice. Whether or not you agree with the exact number, the principle holds that excellence is slow and takes work that most people never see.

Of course, the road isn't smooth. Hustle culture tells Gen Z to work harder, grind longer, and measure worth by productivity. But the truth is, that path often leads to burnout. The antidote isn't quitting—it's reframing. You have to see setbacks as stepping stones, not as failures. Every rejection, every redirection, every detour is raw material for growth.

That mindset—embrace the suck—means accepting that the challenging, unglamorous moments are the ones that forge the skills you'll rely on later.

The truth is that different generations bring different strengths. Boomers were taught loyalty and patience—the value of staying the course. My Gen X peers learned resilience and the ability to pivot when doors closed. Even Millennials have brought their own value to the world with their focus on innovation, the side hustle mentality, and a willingness to disrupt. Each perspective matters. Each one can guide Gen Z as they carve their own path forward.

Let me share a personal experience of my own. In my final year as an Air Force ROTC cadet, I had a commandant of cadets who simply did not like me. At the time, getting a good first assignment wasn't like it is today, with websites and career counselors who can walk you through the process. We didn't have that level of access or transparency. Instead, I had to go to the library and sift through microfiche—those little transparent sheets of film that stored old newspaper clippings and job postings. The information was often outdated by months, if not years. Ultimately, the most significant factor in getting a good assignment came down to whether your commandant would advocate for you. Mine wasn't interested in helping.

I graduated with a physics degree, hoping to be assigned to Systems Command in Los Angeles. Instead, I got the 27th Supply Squadron at Cannon AFB, in a very remote part of eastern New Mexico. It wasn't what I wanted, nor a career field with much potential. But it gave me something else: *leadership experience*. I was one of seven officers overseeing more than 300 enlisted Airmen. Compare that to a second lieutenant in space operations, who might have been one of two officers on a small crew. I learned how to lead people—how to manage, mentor, and make decisions with real consequences.

Still, I knew I needed to leave Supply if I wanted a meaningful long-term career. The only way was to volunteer for a hardship assignment: a one-year tour on the Distant Early Warning (DEW) Line, 200 miles north of the Arctic Circle. I became a quality assurance evaluator for remote radar sites spanning from Alaska to Greenland. I lived out of a suitcase, worked in 40-below temperatures, and spent weeks isolated in desolate locations.

Would I want to do it again? Absolutely not. But would I trade the experience? Not for anything. Not only did it get me back on track with Space Command, but it also became one of the most incredible learning experiences of my life. It forced me to embrace the suck, adapt to harsh environments, and grow in ways I could never have anticipated. That detour, unpleasant as it was, gave me skills that carried me through the rest of my career.

Fast forward a generation, and I saw my son, Julian, face a different kind of setback.

Julian was a talented athlete with a real shot at playing college football. As a freshman, he kicked on varsity. As a sophomore, he was the backup varsity quarterback. By his junior year, he was all-conference; he came into his senior year as a returning starting QB, with Division I teams keeping an eye on him. He had talent, yes, but he also had the work ethic. For years, he had committed to putting in the effort: long hours in the gym, serious training regimens, extra sessions with coaches. He lived the 10,000-hour principle, pouring hundreds of hours into the craft monthly.

Then, the week before his senior season opener, tragedy struck. During a scrimmage, the coaches failed to put a red shirt on him—a signal to protect your key player. On the second play, an all-state defensive lineman drove him into the turf. Julian's clavicle dislocated, pinning against an artery. X-rays revealed the risk was so severe that he needed emergency surgery with a cardiothoracic surgeon on standby. He developed a blood clot, and for three months, I had to administer blood-thinning shots twice a day to prevent it from turning fatal. His senior season was over before it began.

Physically, he recovered. But mentally, the injury, followed by the disruption of COVID, left him adrift. Division II offers were still on the table, but the Division I opportunities vanished. Football, the dream we had invested years in, was gone.

At 21, Julian faced another crossroads. His solar sales career wasn't working out, and he started discussing a new path—becoming a pilot. He asked me to co-sign an $80,000 loan to get through flight school in nine months. I wasn't convinced. Maybe I had gone in on his football dream too eagerly, and I wasn't ready to bankroll another uncertain pursuit.

But Julian proved me wrong. He took $10,000 of his own money, earned his private pilot's license, and showed he was serious. That changed everything. I helped him access his college fund, and he enrolled in a program that allowed him to use his 529 to cover costs. He's the senior instructor at a flight school in Greeley, Colorado, today. He has already been accepted into a major airline's intern program. He's not done—he's just getting started—but I couldn't be prouder.

And you know what struck me most? Watching him in the cockpit was like watching him on the football field again: focused, coachable, and mastering a craft under pressure. Football didn't define his destiny, but it shaped the resilience, discipline, and determination he now carries into aviation. All those hours, all that effort—it was never wasted. It was just redirected. Another life lesson in disguise.

The lesson for Gen X and Gen Z is the same: *success rarely looks how you expect it to.* The detours, the disappointments, the losses—they aren't wasted. They're the forge. They're where patience is tested, resilience is built, and strength is earned.

Lasting success doesn't happen overnight. It occurs in the suck, in the grind, in the detours you didn't choose but learned from anyway.

If there's one truth, I hope you carry forward from this chapter, it's this: *lasting success is never fast, but it is always real.*

The myth of overnight success tempts us because it looks effortless. It promises shortcuts and easy wins. But as both

Gen X and Gen Z stories show, the setbacks, the reroutes, and the long stretches of effort forge the character you'll rely on when things get hard.

When I look at my son Julian's journey, I see that lesson come to life. His football dream ended in an instant—with a violent tackle, an emergency surgery, and months of painful recovery. On the surface, it looked like wasted years, like everything he had worked for had been stolen from him. But in reality, those hours in the gym, those years of training, that discipline of pushing himself—none of it was wasted. It all came back, just in a different arena. When he stepped into the cockpit, he brought the same focus, resilience, and determination that once drove him on the football field.

That's the more profound truth: *success doesn't always appear where you expect it.* Sometimes the path you've been training for ends abruptly, but the skills, the mindset, and the resilience you built don't disappear. They wait for the next opportunity. And when it comes, you're ready in ways you couldn't have imagined.

So, here's my challenge to Gen Z and anyone chasing that elusive "big break": *commit to the long game.* Pick one area of your life—whether it's your career, your craft, or your personal growth—and give it five years of consistent effort before you judge whether it's working. Not five weeks, not five months—five years. That's how you build the foundation that actually lasts.

And when you hit the inevitable obstacles—and you will—don't see them as wasted time. See them as part of the forge. That's where you're learning the resilience, the adaptability, and the patience that will make your eventual success sustainable.

Because the real myth of overnight success isn't just that it's rare. It's that it's even desirable. The truth is the best success stories—the ones that endure—are written over years of persistence and struggle.

Julian didn't become a pilot in a flash. I didn't build my career without detours. Nirvana didn't make it big without years of unseen grind. And you won't either. But when the moment comes—when your preparation meets opportunity—you'll be ready.

So, embrace the suck. Stay the course. Keep climbing uphill. Success may not come fast, but it will be yours to keep when it comes.

---

[1] *Harvard Business Review* article titled **"Why Start ups Fail,"** by Tom Eisenmann, published in the May–June 2021 issue

[2] "The Rise and Fall of the Dot Com Bubble," Investopedia, updated April 2024.

[3] "The Rise and Fall of TikTok Influencers," Forbes, 2022.

[4] Taylor Lorenz, "How MrBeast Became Successful on YouTube," The New York Times, 2019.

[5] Linsay Ellis and Aaron Zitner, "*Americans Lose Faith That Hard Work Leads to Economic Gains, WSJ-NORC Poll Finds*", The Wall Street Journal, Sep 1, 2025.

[6] Willa Bennett, "*How Did Noah Beck Become the Biggest TikTok Guy on Earth?*", GQ Magazine, 19 August 2021.

Chapter 3: Digital vs. Real-Life Connection

Navigating the balance between online and in-person relationships, avoiding social media pitfalls, and maintaining meaningful human connections.

Why do so many still feel isolated in a world where you can "connect" with thousands of people online? Gen Z knows this tension better than anyone. You've grown up with the internet, not as a tool you adopted but as the air you breathe. Your earliest friendships may have started on messaging apps or gaming platforms. You might maintain daily streaks on Snapchat or send more texts in a day than your parents made phone calls in a month. Online communities are everywhere—on TikTok, Discord, Instagram, and beyond. And in many ways, this digital network is incredible: it lets you share your creativity instantly, discover people who share your niche interests, and maintain connections across distances that used to kill friendships.

But here's the catch: while digital connection offers speed, reach, and convenience, it often struggles to deliver depth. The "likes" may roll in, but do they leave you feeling seen? The group chat might buzz, but does it make you feel truly known? Research has shown that heavy social media use can increase feelings of loneliness and anxiety, particularly when relationships remain shallow or overly curated. The paradox is striking: the most connected generation in history also reports record levels of disconnection.

Take, for example, a 2018 study published in the *Journal of Social and Clinical Psychology*. Researchers found that college students who limited social media use to just 30 minutes a day reported significant decreases in loneliness and depression after three weeks[1]. The case was clear: it wasn't that social media was inherently bad, but that overreliance on digital connection without in-person grounding left students emotionally drained. Limiting online time nudged them toward deeper, real-world engagement, improving their mental health.

Gen X understands this tension from a different angle. We grew up forming friendships before the internet was woven into daily life. As teenagers, we flocked to the shopping mall. We'd stroll the stores, catch a movie (keep in mind in those days there was no NETFLIX, most TVs had only four or five channels, and HBO was just becoming a thing), grab food or a drink at the food court, and look to run into others our age —kind of like the physical version of a chat room. Even in rural parts of Oklahoma, there was an equivalent. It was called cruising: you'd drive from one side of town to another, turning around at the Sonic drive-through or the QuikTrip gas station. Once you've found your friends, you'd head to the river or lake to socialize. Relationships were built face-to-face, through unplanned conversations, long walks home from school, or weekends spent just hanging out. Then, in adulthood, we watched as digital communication transformed everything—first with email, then chatrooms, then social media. We had to learn how to navigate this new landscape, balancing the efficiency of online connection with the authenticity of in-person presence.

That's the challenge and the opportunity in front of you. This chapter explores how to balance the digital and the real. We'll look at the lessons Gen X learned when the internet arrived, how those lessons apply today, and what strategies you can use to ensure your connections aren't just wide, but meaningful.

For Gen X, connection was rooted in physical presence. If you wanted to hang out with your friends, you had to show up at their house, call their landline (and maybe survive a slightly awkward conversation with their parents first), or walk the neighborhood until you found them. Texting wasn’t a thing yet, and neither were personal cell phones. We piggybacked on our parents’ landlines, which meant everyone in the household knew who you were calling and how long you stayed on the line. Privacy was limited, but that was part of the deal.

Friendships were forged through countless small, in-person moments: sitting on the front steps talking until the streetlights came on, passing notes in class, or spending Saturdays riding bikes with no destination in mind. When I lived in Santa Clara County, I took the bus by myself at 12. That meant learning to read a bus schedule and a map—skills you picked up quickly if you wanted to see your friends. On the other hand, when I lived in rural Oklahoma, the bus wasn’t even an option. Instead, I’d walk a mile to the closest friend’s house. Truth be told, in a farm setting, it wasn’t unusual in the 80s to see 13- and 14-year-olds driving tractors or dirt bikes down the county dirt roads to meet up. Each place had its advantages and disadvantages, but the point was the same: connection required effort, planning, and showing up in person.

The mall became our social hub in the late 80s and early 90s. It wasn’t just a place to shop — it was where you went to see and be seen. We’d wander the food court with sodas in hand, browse cassette tapes at the record store, or meet at the movie theater for the latest blockbuster. In many ways, the mall functioned like today’s group chat: a central gathering point where conversations unfolded, relationships deepened, and sometimes even drama played out.

In smaller towns, the ritual looked a little different. We had “cruising.” You’d drive back and forth through the main strip of town — past the Sonic drive-in, the convenience store, or the movie theater — hoping to spot your friends doing the same. Eventually, you'd pull over, park, and turn a random evening into a memory. Looking back, these rituals were essentially the analog version of logging on. Instead of checking notifications, you checked who was out on the strip that night.

When digital technology finally arrived, it didn't replace those connections overnight. At first, it was an add-on. Email sped up communication, pagers gave us a taste of instant contact, and eventually, the first chatrooms on AOL or Yahoo opened the door to meeting people we might never see face-to-face. For many of us, the transition felt exciting but also disorienting. Suddenly, you could "talk" to someone nationwide with a dial-up modem. The novelty was undeniable — but the depth wasn't the same as piling into a friend's car and staying out too late.

Gen X also learned that digital tools carried risks. While I could appreciate the evolution from landlines to flip phones to today's smartphones, it's impossible not to feel the loss of personal connection — and the growing concern of being constantly monitored and tracked by the devices we carry everywhere. Email brought its own hard lessons: many a career was cut short or made painfully awkward because someone hit "send" before realizing what they had written. Then came Facebook. At first, the novelty of sharing your life with friends and family felt like a revolution in connection. But I also know more than one family that dissolved after an affair began through social media. The very tool meant to bring people closer together sometimes pulled them apart.

Gen X quickly learned that digital communication is a tool, not a replacement. A 2019 Pew Research Center survey confirmed what many of us had already known: while 81% of Americans say digital technology makes staying in touch easier, most still rank in-person interactions as the most meaningful form of connection[2]. For Gen X, that preference wasn't abstract — it was lived experience. We knew what life felt like before and after the digital shift and could tell the difference.

This unique position — growing up analog, then adapting to digital — gave Gen X a front-row seat to the strengths and weaknesses of both worlds. We embraced the convenience of new technology but also carried forward an instinct to value presence: to recognize that the best memories often come from showing up, not just logging in.

On the surface, Gen X and Gen Z seem to live in entirely different universes regarding connection. One came of age in a world where the internet was a novelty; the other never knew a world without it. Yet beneath those differences, both generations wrestle with the same human need: to belong, to be understood, and to find people who will walk through life with them.

I saw this play out in my own life. I married my first wife in 1995 — the same year Match.com launched as the first major online dating website. Fast forward two decades, after the divorce, and I entered the unfamiliar world of online dating myself. By then, the landscape had exploded. I didn't use the free swiping apps like Tinder or Plenty of Fish; instead, I leaned toward the more traditional sites like eHarmony and Match, where you paid a fee, filled out profiles, and answered long strings of questions. The shift was dramatic. My first marriage had come from the old ways: being introduced by a friend, going to a bar, or just meeting someone through shared circles. Suddenly, it felt like I had access to a firehose of options — a digital catalog of faces and stories.

Like any tool, online dating requires learning. At first, it was overwhelming. But over time, I became more proficient. I learned the importance of honest communication before rushing into a first meeting. When I connected with my current wife, we exchanged emails for nearly two months before we met for coffee one afternoon. That practice of valuing communication over instant gratification made all the difference. In the end, technology didn't replace dating; it enhanced it. What mattered was using the tool with intention instead of being used by it.

My youngest son, Ian, provided me with a window into how Gen Z experiences this same challenge of using technology to foster relationships. Ian relied on us throughout high school to access his cell phone and laptop. That included giving us visibility into his social media accounts, which allowed us to monitor his communications. Despite his many attempts to evade that oversight — downloading alternative apps designed to hide activity from parents — we stayed aware. It left us with a constant dilemma: do we confront him on every misstep, or allow him to think he'd succeeded in getting away with something so we could continue monitoring? We chose the latter, letting him believe he had slipped past us while quietly watching as he learned some hard lessons.

We saw a teenager struggling to find his footing in digital communication. Ian constantly tried to be "cool," to project a digitally sophisticated persona. In reality, he wandered aimlessly, often confused about why he got ghosted or why certain interactions collapsed without warning. Fortunately, he had sports to fall back on. On the athletic field, the rules were clear, the objectives measurable, and the camaraderie genuine. Win or lose, he knew his teammates would be there to share the outcome. That contrast — between the uncertainty of online social life and the groundedness of physical, team-based connection — showed him where authentic belonging could still be found.

Research echoes Ian's experience. A 2024 *Frontiers in Developmental Psychology* study found that adolescents and young people rated online friendships as only "moderately close." However, when those online relationships transitioned into offline, face-to-face interactions, their sense of closeness increased significantly[3]. In other words, digital platforms alone often left teens feeling adrift — just as Ian did — but grounding those connections in real-world experiences, like sports or clubs, made them far more meaningful.

The Similarities

Both generations value community and identity. Gen X found it in neighborhoods, schools, churches, sports teams, and workplaces. Gen Z finds it in online platforms — Discord servers for gamers, TikTok communities for niche interests, Reddit forums for just about everything under the sun. The medium is different, but the impulse is the same: "Where do I fit, and who understands me?"

Both generations also adapted to new communication technologies as they came along. Gen X went from landlines to pagers, pagers to flip phones, flip phones to early social media. Gen Z has watched platforms rise and fall even faster: Vine to TikTok, MySpace to Instagram, Facebook to Snapchat. Every generation of young people learns to master the dominant technology of its time — the difference is how quickly those technologies now turn over.

The Differences

The contrast shows most in how each generation prioritizes connection. For Gen X, digital interaction has always been a supplement. A text, an email, or even a Facebook post was an extra layer on top of in-person relationships. For Gen Z, digital interaction can often feel like the primary layer — where friendships begin, develop, and sometimes even end without crossing into the physical world.

Another difference lies in scale. Gen X friendships tended to be fewer but deeper. You might have had a circle of 5–10 close friends you saw regularly. For Gen Z, social networks can number in the hundreds or even thousands, but the quality of those ties varies. According to a 2022 *Pew Research Center* report, 54% of teens say they have at least one close friend they met online[4]. Yet nearly 60% also admit it can be hard to tell how genuine online connections are. It's a reminder that quantity and quality don't always align.

Mental health is another area where the differences show. Gen X worried about peer pressure, cliques, and being left out of Friday night plans. Gen Z faces those same struggles — but magnified by the constant visibility of social media. FOMO (Fear of Missing Out) isn't just not being invited to the party; it's watching it unfold on Instagram Stories in real time. Research from the American Psychological Association shows that heavy social media users, especially teens, report higher levels of anxiety and depression compared to peers who balance digital and in-person engagement[5].

Bridging the Gap

And yet, both generations share something important: a desire for authenticity. Gen X remembers when "hanging out" meant being present in the same physical space, and we carry that lesson forward. Gen Z, despite growing up digitally native, consistently reports that in-person time with friends is more rewarding than online interaction. In fact, a 2023 *Common Sense Media* survey found that 73% of teens prefer face-to-face time with friends, even though much of their daily interaction still happens online[6].

That's the common ground: Gen X and Gen Z want genuine relationships. The difference lies in how we pursue them — one generation grounded in analog habits, the other fluent in digital environments. The challenge, and the opportunity, is to learn from each other. Through presence and patience, Gen X can share how depth is built over time. Gen Z can teach adaptability and creativity by using new tools to maintain connections across distances. Together, those lessons point toward a hybrid model of connection that honors the best of both worlds.

If there's one lesson Gen X can pass on about connection, it's this: balance matters. Technology isn't the enemy but isn't the complete answer either. The danger comes when digital interaction crowds out the real-life relationships that give you grounding, depth, and resilience. Here are a few practical steps Gen Z can take, drawn from both experience and research:

1. Balance screen time with face time.

It's not about quitting social media — it's about managing it. As previously pointed out by the 2018 *Journal of Social and Clinical Psychology* study that showed reducing social media use to just 30 minutes a day significantly decreased loneliness and depression among college students. Think of it like a diet: too many "junk connections" leave you feeling empty, while a healthier, real-world connection nourishes you. Start small. Pick one night a week to put the phone away and be fully present with friends or family.

2. Prioritize depth over breadth.

Gen X friendships were smaller in number but often stronger in quality. Today's temptation is to measure yourself by your follower count or how many people view your stories. But here's the truth: meaningful relationships aren't built on numbers but on time, trust, and shared experience. Invest more energy in a few friendships that matter instead of spreading yourself thin across dozens of shallow ones.

3. Let digital be the bridge, not the destination.

Use online tools to spark and maintain relationships, but don't stop there. My son Ian discovered that while online interactions often left him confused or ghosted, the camaraderie of the athletic field gave him grounding. Sports, clubs, volunteering, or even a part-time job can create in-person bonds that stick. Take digital conversations offline — grab coffee, study together, or meet for a workout when possible. Research consistently shows that shared real-world activities strengthen emotional bonds in ways digital-only exchanges rarely can.

4. Practice presence.

One of the most straightforward but most powerful habits: when you're with someone, really *be* with them. Put the phone away, make eye contact, and listen without the distraction of notifications. Gen X learned this the hard way. Many careers were damaged in the early days of email because people fired off messages without thinking. We learned to slow down, reflect, and be intentional. You can do the same in relationships. Show people they matter by giving them your full attention.

5. Learn from both worlds.

The advantage of being Gen Z is fluency — you understand digital tools better than anyone. The advantage of Gen X is perspective — we lived both with and without them. Together, these lessons point to a hybrid model of connection. Lean into your digital creativity, but don't lose sight of what's timeless: patience, presence, and persistence.

At the heart of this is a simple truth: the best connections come from effort. Whether it's maintaining a streak, showing up for practice, or making time for a coffee date, relationships deepen when you choose to nurture them. Don't let digital convenience trick you into thinking connection is automatic. It's always intentional.

But the truth be told. I have not always followed my own advice.

I just registered for my 40-year high school reunion. They're getting a taco truck, and we'll gather at a park near the school. It's funny — I missed every reunion before this one because I had fallen completely out of touch with anyone from those days. Honestly, I wouldn't have known about it if my friend Susie from high school hadn't looked me up on LinkedIn a few years ago.

The truth is, I lost contact with almost everyone after graduation. College, the Air Force, moving around the world — each stage of life pulled me further from those friendships. The ones I managed to keep during summers back home faded as new assignments took me elsewhere. Marriage, then kids, became my center of gravity. And when divorce finally stripped that away, I realized how few old ties I had maintained.

That's why Susie finding me again was such a gift. The nostalgia was overwhelming — a reminder of connections I thought were long gone. Ironically, it was technology that brought me back into the fold. LinkedIn, emails, texts, even the annual Christmas letter I put together on my laptop to send out — all these tools reopened doors and rekindled bonds I thought I had lost forever.

It taught me something important: maybe Gen Z, with its instinct to maintain relationships digitally, has something to teach us, too. For all the risks and pitfalls of online connections, they can also preserve the ties that time and distance might otherwise sever. The trick is to let technology serve the relationship, not replace it.

At the end of the day, Gen X and Gen Z share the same human hunger: the need for authentic connection. The tools have changed — from landlines and handwritten notes to Snapchat streaks and TikTok comments — but the essence hasn't. What matters most isn't the platform; it's the presence.

My son Ian learned this lesson the hard way. He tried to project confidence, sophistication, and coolness online, but too often he ended up ghosted or frustrated. On the field, though, he found what he couldn't online: clarity, camaraderie, and the reassurance that his teammates would stand with him, win or lose. His story reminds us that real-life presence grounds us in ways the digital world cannot fully replicate.

And I've lived the lesson myself. I let friendships fade for decades as life pulled me in different directions. Careers, marriage, and kids became a new anchor, but they also crowded out the old ties. When I finally reconnected with friends from high school, it was overwhelming. That reunion wasn't just about nostalgia. It was about rediscovering a part of myself buried under years of busyness and silence. Technology opened the door, but the real joy came from standing in the same park with people who had once shaped my world.

So, here's the challenge: **don't wait for life to remind you what you've lost. Choose today to invest in the connections that matter.** For Gen Z, that might mean moving one online friendship into the real world — invite a friend for coffee, a workout, or a study session instead of just a DM (Direct Message). For Gen X, it might mean reaching out to someone from your past, not with a "like" or a comment, but with a phone call or a plan to meet face-to-face.

Resilient connection takes effort, and it always will. But in that effort — showing up, listening, sharing life — friendships deepen, families strengthen, and communities endure. Whether through the immediacy of a text, the warmth of a Christmas letter, or the laughter shared over tacos at a high school reunion, the truth is the same: **connection thrives when nurtured and lived.**

So, my call to action is simple: **Pick one relationship this week to strengthen intentionally.** Send the text, make the call, or better yet, show up in person. Don't let the noise of the digital world convince you that a "like" is enough. Go beyond the screen. The most lasting connections are never just scrolled through — they're lived.

---

[1] Hunt, M. G., Marx, R., Lipson, C., & Young, J. (2018). *No More FOMO: Limiting Social Media Decreases Loneliness and Depression.* Journal of Social and Clinical Psychology, 37(10), 751–768. https://doi.org/10.1521/jscp.2018.37.10.751

[2] Pew Research Center (2019). *Americans' Trust in Technology and Connection Preferences.* Retrieved from [pewresearch.org].

[3] Al-Jbouri, A., Volk, A. A., Spadafora, N., & Andrews, K. (2024). *How close are our online friends? Perceived*

friendship closeness online versus offline in adolescence. Frontiers in Developmental Psychology, 3:1419756. https://doi.org/10.3389/fdpys.2024.1419756

[4] Pew Research Center (2022). Teens, Social Media, and Technology 2022.

[5] American Psychological Association (2019). Social Media and Mental Health.

[6] Common Sense Media (2023). Teens and Social Connection Report.

Chapter 4: Self-Reliance in a Hyper-Connected World

Cultivating independence, building real-world problem-solving skills, and learning why self-reliance still matters in a hyper-connected world.

We live in a world where nearly every answer is at our fingertips. If a pipe leaks, we can pull up a YouTube tutorial. If we're lost, we can drop a pin on Google Maps. If we need to fix a car or cook a new dish, an endless scroll of AI tools, forums, and videos will guide us. It feels efficient—and often it is—but there's a hidden cost: the gradual erosion of self-reliance.

For Generation X, self-reliance wasn't optional but part of daily life. We grew up before smartphones, before 24/7 access to information, before social networks connected us to thousands of people instantly. When something broke, you either figured out how to fix it or went without. When you got lost, you unfolded a paper map or asked someone for directions. When parents were at work, latchkey kids learned to care for themselves, make meals, and handle problems.

Nothing captures that spirit better than my first truck: a black 1974 Ford F-150 with a manual transmission. Most Gen Z will never know the feeling of driving with all four limbs engaged—left hand on the steering wheel, right hand on the gear shift, left foot on the clutch, and right foot on the accelerator—cutting up a dirt road and feeling the back tires slide, pretending I was Bo Duke on the back roads of Cherokee County. Trucks back then were simple machines, not loaded with computers or emissions equipment. At sixteen, I spent an entire weekend under that truck replacing a worn clutch plate—not because I was a mechanic, but because I couldn't afford one. If I wanted transportation, I had to learn to maintain it myself.

That knowledge saved me more than once. I remember driving to Muskogee with a couple of buddies when the battery died, leaving us stranded late at night with no cell phones to call for help. A dead battery matters because it provides the electrical charge needed to turn the starter motor, which cranks the engine to life. With a manual transmission, you can bypass the starter by "popping the clutch." Here's how it worked: I put the truck in neutral and held down the clutch while my friends pushed. Once we gained enough momentum, I released the clutch with the shift already in first gear. The forward motion turned the engine over, and the truck roared back to life. We limped home, proud that we had solved the problem ourselves.

The point wasn't just saving money—the resilience came from knowing we could get out of a tough spot without anyone else's help.

Today's environment is the opposite: unlimited connection, constant access, and near-instant solutions. That abundance makes life easier, but it also risks making us dependent. Gen Z has incredible tools, but sometimes those tools do the heavy lifting that builds resilience, creativity, and problem-solving muscles.

In this chapter, we'll explore why Gen X thrived on independence, why problem-solving skills still matter in the real world, and how you can build confidence from knowing you can rely on yourself—even when the Wi-Fi signal drops.

For Generation X, independence wasn't an abstract value—it was the air we breathed. We came of age in a world that demanded we figure things out for ourselves, often without much guidance or a safety net. Technology hadn't yet closed the gap between questions and answers, so problem-solving required creativity, patience, and resilience.

Many of us were **latchkey kids**, coming home from school to empty houses. Parents worked long hours, and we learned early how to make meals, manage chores, and handle problems independently. If the TV antenna broke, you adjusted it until the picture came in. If the bike chain snapped, you flipped it over in the driveway and fixed it with greasy fingers. There wasn't always an adult—or an internet forum—ready to bail you out.

That environment didn't make us exceptional mechanics, chefs, or survivalists. It made us resourceful. The lesson wasn't that you had to be an expert in everything, but that you had to be willing to try. Even failure was a teacher. Every problem we solved, whether patching a tube on a bicycle or figuring out how to stretch a paycheck through the end of the month, built confidence in our ability to adapt.

It isn't easy to describe what it truly meant to be a resilient Gen Xer. It's better explained through personal stories. For me, one moment stands out. I already had my Air Force commission the summer after graduating from college. Still, my reporting date was seven months away. I decided to pack my Honda Prelude and drive from Silicon Valley back to Oklahoma to spend one last season at my old stomping grounds before beginning my military career. I had maybe $300 to my name. Gas in 1990 was about $1.20 a gallon. After twenty-three hours on the road, I pulled into Tahlequah without incident—but essentially broke.

But Tahlequah wasn't the same as I remembered. My mom and stepfather had divorced, so I no longer had a house to return to. Most of my friends had moved on—some to bigger cities like Tulsa, and others were already married and had kids. We didn't have Facebook to keep tabs on everyone; we just went to Wal-Mart and saw who was around. I showed up with a *we'll see who's still here* attitude. The problem was, I didn't have enough money to drive back to California, let alone a place to stay while I was there. I did what Gen Xers did: I figured it out. Within a few days, I landed a job at the local Pizza Hut, found a spare room with a couch to rent, and started working to earn enough money for the next chapter of my life—first back to California, then on to my first assignment in Clovis, New Mexico.

Now, to a Gen Zer, this might seem reckless or naïve. But to me, the situation never felt unreasonable. I wanted to do something before entering active duty, so I made the choice and trusted myself to handle whatever came up. That was the Gen X mindset: leap first, figure out the landing on the way down.

I remember one particular week when I had just two dollars left in my wallet and three days before my first Pizza Hut paycheck. For those three days, I lived on twelve-cent packets of Top Ramen. It wasn't glamorous, but it worked. And it left me with a permanent lesson: I never wanted to be that broke again. Adversity didn't crush me; it taught me. It didn't make me a victim; it made me stronger.

The result was a generation that thrived on self-reliance. We didn't necessarily seek out independence—it was placed on us by circumstance and often by our own choices. But in hindsight, that constant practice of solving our own problems became one of the defining traits of Gen X. It shaped us into adults who could adapt to uncertainty, embrace new challenges, and keep moving forward even when the way ahead wasn't clear.

For Gen Z, the same situation might unfold differently. Instead of packing up a car and driving cross-country on little more than instinct and a few hundred dollars, today's default response might be to crowdsource advice, Google solutions, or post a plea for help on social media. The tools at their disposal are powerful, but they also change the instinct. Where Gen X often said, *"I'll figure it out,"* Gen Z is more likely to ask, *"Who can figure this out for me?"*

And that's where the gap begins—the difference between resilience built through scarcity and resilience tested by abundance.

At first glance, the gap between Gen X and Gen Z seems like a canyon—one defined by technology, culture, and pace of life. Yet beneath the surface, there are some surprising similarities. Both generations have been shaped by uncertainty, disruption, and the need to adapt quickly to changing circumstances.

For both Gen X and Gen Z, uncertainty was a constant. Gen X grew up in the shadow of the Cold War, economic recessions, and shifting family structures. Gen Z faces pandemics, inflation, climate anxiety, and political division. In both cases, stability felt fragile. Gen X and Gen Z each have a desire for independence. Just as Gen X wanted to break free from hovering institutions and figure things out alone, many Gen Zers value side hustles, entrepreneurial paths, and carving out identities beyond traditional systems. There also appears to be a resilience-when-tested trait for each. When systems fail—whether it's a global pandemic or a broken-down car—both generations find ways to adapt, often using different tools.

However, there are differences, for example, in the information environment. Gen X had a scarcity of information; we relied on libraries, word of mouth, or trial and error. Gen Z is buried under an overabundance of information—algorithms, search results, and social feeds. One generation had to work hard to find answers; the other must work hard to filter truth from noise. There's also a difference in what I would call each generation's problem-solving instinct. Gen X defaulted to *"I'll figure it out"* because often there was no one else. Gen Z, raised with instant access, tends toward *"I'll look it up"* or *"Who can help me?"* Both instincts can solve problems—but one builds deeper self-reliance, while the other risks outsourcing it.

Why is this important? Because when systems collapse, self-reliance matters. Take **Hurricane Katrina in 2005**. Thousands were stranded without functioning infrastructure, reliable communication, or immediate government response. Survival often depended on improvisation, neighbors helping neighbors, and grassroots efforts rather than top-down rescue. Similarly, during the **Texas Freeze of February 2021**, millions lost power, heat, and water in below-freezing temperatures. Technology and modern infrastructure failed spectacularly. Families who knew how to insulate pipes, cook on camping stoves, or pool resources with neighbors fared better than those who assumed the system would always work. The lesson is clear: in moments of crisis, apps and posts don't save people—ingenuity, old-fashioned problem-solving, and community resilience do.

On a personal note, I lived in the nearby Florida Panhandle the year before Katrina. That year, my town of Navarre was hit not by one but two hurricanes: **Ivan** and **Dennis**. Ivan, a Category 4 storm, brought a 12-foot surge that devastated the Emerald Coast. Being new to hurricanes, I followed the local base's direction and evacuated my family to Augusta, Georgia. Two days later, I returned home alone to assess the damage—and it was like stepping into another world.

A hundred miles out along I-65, FEMA trucks were staging with equipment to rebuild the power grid. Sixty miles out, I began seeing tornado damage—trees down across roads, already being cleared by local crews. The last ten miles into Navarre took over an hour. At the junction of County Highway 87 and State Highway 98, near the water, the waves erased an entire apartment complex, leaving behind a pile of debris. When I finally reached my neighborhood, the scene was surreal: the sound of dozens of diesel generators humming like a go-kart track, neighbors already cleaning debris, and people cheerfully inviting each other to cookouts before their frozen meat spoiled.

We were far enough inland to avoid storm surge, but nearly every roof took damage. Thousands of homes were covered in blue tarps. Yet there was no panic. Gas pumps restarted within a day, power returned within three, and stores reopened shortly after. Unlike the chaos in New Orleans during Katrina, our community leaned into resilience. No looting, no violence—just neighbors helping neighbors. To this day, I wonder why two regions devastated by hurricanes had such different outcomes. The only answer I can find is resilience: one community had it deeply ingrained, the other did not.

Another critical difference between the generations lies in the role of failure. Gen X was used to trial and error because failure was unavoidable. You tried, you stumbled, and you learned. Gen Z can often avoid failure with tutorials, walkthroughs, and AI-generated solutions. That efficiency saves time but can also rob them of the growth that comes from struggle. Then there are the differences in social connections. Gen X friendships often depended on physical proximity—you knew who was around because you saw them at the store, school, or church. Gen Z has constant digital networks, but paradoxically, it often struggles with a deeper connection.

Yet, there is reason for optimism. When tested, Gen Z rises. Programs like **FIRST Robotics[1]**, which challenge students to design, build, and program robots under strict time constraints, consistently demonstrate how Gen Z thrives when placed in real-world problem-solving environments. These competitions demand persistence, teamwork, and creativity—the same traits Gen X developed through scarcity. Likewise, **college startup incubators[2]** allow young entrepreneurs to turn ideas into viable businesses, often with limited resources and steep learning curves. In both cases, Gen Z proves that, given the right environment, they are more than capable of adapting and excelling.

The contrast isn't about one generation being "better" than the other. It's about recognizing that self-reliance built through scarcity and self-reliance tested by abundance are not the same. Gen X learned confidence by necessity; Gen Z must be more intentional about developing it.

The lessons of self-reliance aren't just history—they're tools Gen Z can use today. The point isn't to live like it's 1985, but to build confidence and adaptability from solving problems without always leaning on instant answers. Here are a few ways to start:

1. Practice crisis thinking before the crisis comes.

When Hurricane Ivan tore through the Florida Panhandle, survival didn't come from panic—it came from preparation and neighbors pulling together. People who already knew how to handle small crises—running generators, cooking without power, having shelf-stable food and water purification systems on hand for emergencies—were the ones who steadied the community. For Gen Z, the lesson is clear: practice small forms of self-reliance now so that when the "big one" hits, you don't freeze. Learn how to shut off a water main, cook with limited tools, or manage a day without your phone or Uber Eats. Small skills build confidence, and confidence builds resilience.

Our culture often labels self-reliant people as "preppers" or "doomsdayers." In reality, many of these people have built up impressive survival skills that usually prove useful in everyday situations—power outages, weather emergencies, or even pandemics. We don't hesitate to buy insurance policies for our homes, cars, or lives. Why not invest in a bit of an insurance policy for ourselves by learning gardening, canning, or other skills that can carry us through temporary hardship?

2. Embrace failure as a teacher.

Gen X learned by trial and error because failure was unavoidable. Gen Z has tools to bypass failure, but in doing so, they sometimes miss the growth that comes with it. Robotics competitions like **FIRST Robotics** prove how powerful failure can be when embraced. Teams often spend weeks building a robot, only to have it break down in the first test. Instead of giving up, they redesign, rebuild, and improve —learning far more than they would have by getting it perfect the first time.

Instead of measuring yourself by pass/fail outcomes, measure by progress. Incorporate failure into your career plan. For example, I once dreamed of becoming an astronaut. I planned to be an Air Force pilot, then a test pilot, and finally, an astronaut. But flying didn't come as naturally as I hoped. While I was skilled at the mechanics, I struggled with situational awareness—airspeed, altitude, and tracking other aircraft in my area. After busting a check ride in Hondo, Texas, I was offered the chance to try again, but I declined. I knew I'd only ever be a below-average pilot, not one of the best. Still, I didn't abandon my dream of space. Instead, I pivoted—applying what I learned about flight training to space training. That decision made me the leading instructional analysis and design expert within today's Space Force.

I often say: if you aim for the fence, you may land in the mud. But if you aim for the moon, you'll clear the fence. I didn't make it into space—but I cleared the fence, and then some. That's a lesson worth living by.

3. Build real-world problem-solving muscles.

The instinct to Google a solution is efficient, but efficiency doesn't always equal growth. Try tackling at least one challenge a week without relying on online shortcuts. Cook a meal from scratch without YouTube. Change a flat tire. Budget your money with a notebook and a calculator. These exercises force you to think, adapt, and trust your judgment.

Ultimately, you're building self-confidence and creating a skill set you'll never regret having. After Katrina, I studied the differences between those paralyzed by crisis and those who thrived during Ivan. What stood out wasn't stockpiles of guns or hidden bunkers—it was skills. First aid, CPR, camping, hunting, and gardening are transferable abilities that help you in everyday life and empower you to assist others in emergencies. That's the essence of real-world resilience.

4. Strengthen your social network—the old-fashioned way.

The neighbors in Navarre, after Hurricane Ivan, didn't wait for FEMA; they leaned on each other. Barbecues, borrowed tools, shared generators—resilience was a community project. Digital networks are powerful, but they're no substitute for real-world connections. For Gen Z, that means cultivating relationships where you live: knowing your neighbors, building trust, and being willing to lend a hand.

Consider this: Who would you rely on if the Wi-Fi went down tomorrow? Preppers often cite a striking fact—modern grocery stores carry only 3–4 days of inventory, compared to two weeks or more fifty years ago. If hit with a surge, a supply chain disruption could leave shelves bare in hours. We saw it happen with toilet paper and sanitizer during COVID-19. When that happens, it's not your online followers who will help—it's your neighbors.

5. Channel creativity into independence.

One of Gen Z's greatest strengths is creativity—coding, content creation, and startups. The key is to channel that creativity into independence. The same spark that fuels a TikTok channel can build a side hustle. The same ingenuity that powers a robotics project can fix real-world problems at home or in your community.

I learned this firsthand when I was stuck in eastern New Mexico, assigned to a supply squadron. It wasn't where I wanted to be, but I got creative. At the time, under General Merrill McPeak, the Air Force was pushing for a volunteer for every position. Few wanted to volunteer for remote posts—especially one 200 miles north of the Arctic Circle. I applied for the assignment, and that decision eventually allowed me to cross-train back into Space Command before becoming a captain. It wasn't luck—it was creativity channeled toward independence, and it got me back to where I wanted to be.

Framework for Problem-Solving

Self-reliance can feel overwhelming until you see it as a process. A simple framework I've picked up as an analyst can guide you through almost any challenge:

- **Define** the problem clearly.
- **Test** a solution with the tools you have.
- **Fail** without shame—it's part of the process.
- **Adjust** based on what you learn.
- **Succeed** by persisting until you get it right.

This framework is timeless. Think of **Apollo 13**, when engineers on the ground and astronauts in space faced a life-threatening crisis with limited tools and materials. Their process was precisely this: define the problem, test solutions, fail and adjust, and eventually succeed. That same problem-solving mindset is available to you—even if your crisis is a flat tire, a lost job, or a personal setback.

The core lesson is that self-reliance is like a muscle. It only grows when it's exercised, tested, and sometimes strained. The hurricanes proved that communities survive because individuals are prepared to act. Robotics competitions prove that the next generation thrives when challenged. For Gen Z, the task is simple: put yourself in situations where you must figure things out, learn from failure, and trust your resourcefulness.

Self-reliance isn't about rejecting technology or pretending the modern world doesn't exist. It's about knowing that when the lights go out, when the network fails, or when life throws something unexpected at you, you won't freeze. You'll move. You'll act. You'll figure it out.

For Gen X, self-reliance was never a philosophy but a way of life. We didn't always get it right, but every time we solved a problem ourselves, we added another layer of confidence and resilience. That's the same muscle Gen Z can build today.

I go back to my first truck, that old black ’74 Ford F-150 with a manual transmission. One night, after the battery died, my buddies and I were stranded in the dark, miles from home with no way to call for help. There was no cell phone, no roadside assistance, no app to bail us out. But I knew my truck well enough to know the workaround. With my friends pushing, I shifted into gear and let momentum bring the engine back to life. We didn’t just get home that night—we learned a lesson: resourcefulness can get you moving again when it feels like everything has stopped.

That’s the image I want you to carry with you. Life will hand you dead batteries—moments where your plans stall and nothing works as it should. Technology may not always have the answer. But if you know how to “pop the clutch”—to draw on the confidence, creativity, and resilience you’ve built—you can get yourself moving again.

So, here’s the challenge: this week, find one problem you’d normally solve with your phone, your parents, or a quick online search—and figure it out yourself. It doesn’t matter how small it is. Cook a meal without looking up a recipe. Fix something in your apartment. Get where you’re going without GPS. Whatever it is, practice relying on your own resourcefulness.

Because one day, when the stakes are higher, it won’t be an app that saves you—it’ll be you. And just like that old Ford, you can jump-start yourself back into motion, no matter how dead the battery seems.

---

[1] *FIRST Inspires (2024)* — “FIRST Longitudinal Study Final Report.” FIRST® (For Inspiration and Recognition of Science and Technology), 2024. Key findings include that 83% of FIRST alumni declare a STEM major by their fourth year in college.

[2] *Kauffman Foundation (2023)* — Cosgrove, B., Gaskin, P., Goff, T., Kenney, E., Milli, J., & Vassell, H. “Access to

Capital for Entrepreneurs: Removing Barriers – 2023 Update." Ewing Marion Kauffman Foundation, June 27, 2023.

Chapter 5: Dealing with Failure and Rejection

Turning rejection into resilience: why setbacks forge stronger character than easy wins ever could.

Failure and rejection sting. They bruise pride, shake confidence, and can leave you questioning your worth. But they also shape character in ways success never could. Every generation faces disappointment—missed opportunities, broken relationships, and lost chances. What defines us is not whether we stumble but what we do after we hit the ground.

For me, that truth became painfully real in 2014—the worst year of my life. I had just been laid off from my job at Orbital Science. It wasn't because of poor performance; I had successfully brought on a new training program for a classified space program. But when the follow-on work never materialized, the position disappeared. I stared at a future without a handsome paycheck. But unlike when I was twenty-three, with little to no responsibility, living on a couch in rural Oklahoma, I now had three school-aged boys and a spouse relying on me. Fortunately, I still had my Air Force reserve job to cushion the blow, but it wasn't enough to sustain a family long term. What then?

I decided to take control back. I was tired of the defense industry, of watching people in high authority being good at surviving failure instead of solving problems. I turned to something familiar. I had put myself through college cooking and even managing restaurants in the '80s—why not try again? I borrowed $10,000 from my father-in-law, bought a struggling coffee shop, and threw myself into small business ownership.

Setting up the shop was the easy part. What I wasn't prepared for was the theft, laziness, and lack of work ethic from employees I genuinely wanted to help. My vision was simple: get the business running, share profits with employees, and eventually step back and let the employees run the business once a better defense job arose. I would give them the opportunity I wished someone had given me. But instead of partnership, I saw deceit—employees stealing cash, handing out free food, and driving away my few dependable workers. They didn't understand, or perhaps didn't care, how much I had invested.

As the business limped along, another blow landed. My wife of nineteen years confessed to me that she *wasn't happy anymore*. That revelation was followed by the discovery of her drug use, adultery, and over a dozen maxed-out credit cards. Creditors soon began knocking on my door. Divorce followed. Bankruptcy came next. We closed the coffee shop, and for the first time in my life, I found myself staring into the abyss—contemplating suicide.

What stopped me were my three sons. No matter how low I had fallen, they needed a father who would keep going. But in 2014, at 47 years old, I felt like a complete failure: laid off, broke, divorced, and with no clear path forward—rock bottom.

That's the thing about failure—it strips you bare, but it also forces you to decide who you will be when there's nothing left to hide behind.

For Gen Z, the sting of rejection often comes wrapped in new packaging. Rejection can feel foreign- or catastrophic in a world of instant feedback, social media likes, and carefully curated online identities. When everyone else's life looks perfect, setbacks can seem like proof you're falling behind.

Add to that the reality of a volatile job market, rising costs of living, and shifting social expectations, and resilience is no longer just helpful—it's a survival skill.

This chapter will explore how Gen X grew up in a different landscape, one where rejection wasn't hidden or softened by participation trophies. We'll examine how our generation learned to take "no" in stride, why rejection is not the opposite of success but part of the same path, and what lessons we can carry forward today. Along the way, we'll see how failure can be reframed as feedback, how rejection often becomes redirection, and why the ability to bounce back stronger is the true measure of resilience.

Gen X was forged in an environment where failure wasn't cushioned. We grew up when report cards arrived in the mail, coaches posted cut lists outside the gym, and rejection letters appeared weeks, if not months, later in your mailbox. There were no participation trophies for simply showing up. If you didn't make the team, you sat in the bleachers. If you didn't get the job, you waited for the next chance.

That doesn't mean failure was easy. It meant we learned to absorb the sting, adjust, and keep moving. That lesson was tested in 2014, when I lived through the triple blow of a layoff, a failed business, and a divorce.

My layoff from Orbital Science was almost a textbook Gen X experience. I had done my job well—successfully building a new training program—but the follow-on work never came, and the company had no choice but to let me go. That story echoed across the generation. During the early '90s "peace dividend" defense drawdowns, tens of thousands of engineers, program managers, and contractors lost their jobs. Later, the 2008 financial crisis hit Gen X especially hard. By some estimates, workers like me in our 40s lost nearly **45% of their wealth between 2007 and 2010[1]**. The lesson was clear: performance didn't guarantee security, and stability could disappear overnight.

By contrast, Baby Boomers—who entered the workforce in the post-WWII boom years—benefited from strong unions, plentiful pensions, and the long economic expansion of the 1950s and 1960s. Where Boomers were nurtured in prosperity, Gen X was often left blindsided by the lack of stability when establishing a career.

When I tried to reinvent myself as a small business owner, I was drawing on the self-reliance that defined Gen X. We grew up with the idea that if you wanted something done right, you did it yourself. Owning a coffee shop was a way to regain control and build something on my own terms. However, within a year, the business folded under the weight of theft, poor employee work ethic, and slim margins. My story wasn't unique. National data shows that about **20% of new small businesses fail within the first year and roughly 50% close within five years[2]**. Gen X learned firsthand that the American dream of entrepreneurship often came with brutal odds.

For Boomers, many of whom launched businesses in the booming 1980s, conditions were often more favorable—easier access to credit, lower startup costs relative to wages, and a growing middle class with disposable income. These generational experiences also shaped political leanings. Boomers, raised in an era of abundance, often saw little harm in devoting energy and resources to social causes—their prosperity made such generosity feel less costly. Gen X, by contrast, came of age in tougher times. We learned the hard way that every paycheck mattered. As a result, we've tended to be more skeptical about easily parting with hard-earned wages in the name of broader social spending.

And then came the collapse of my marriage. For many Gen Xers, like me, divorce was part of the cultural landscape—we grew up during the divorce surge of the '70s and '80s, when rates doubled nationally. By midlife, nearly **46% of Gen Xers who had ever married eventually divorced[3]**. That was the reality we inherited: almost half of marriages ended in dissolution. Still, nothing prepared me for the betrayal, financial ruin, and personal devastation that followed nineteen years of marriage. I lost my job, business, savings, and family in one year. Rock bottom wasn't a phrase anymore—it was my daily reality.

Gen X learned resilience because we had no choice. We weren't handed safety nets or easy do-overs. We had to figure out what to do with the pieces left after life fell apart. That meant swallowing pride, facing creditors, raising my three sons, and slowly building back from nothing.

This perspective—accepting rejection as part of the process—is what sets Gen X apart from our Baby Boomer predecessors. Boomers were shaped by prosperity, but Gen X was shaped by instability. We didn't expect life to be fair, but we came to believe it could still be meaningful if we kept going. That belief transformed my worst year into the beginning of a different kind of strength.

On the surface, Gen X and Gen Z may seem worlds apart—one raised on mixtapes and pay phones, the other on TikTok and smartphones. However, when it comes to failure and rejection, the experiences are more connected than they first appear. Both generations have been tested by job loss, failed ventures, and broken relationships. The difference lies in how those struggles arrive, their processing, and their context.

Job Loss and Layoffs

Gen X came of age in the defense drawdowns of the 1990s and weathered the Great Recession of 2008. Layoffs were often slow, painful, and highly visible—you got a letter, your name was on a list, and your career trajectory could change overnight.

Gen Z faces similar instability but often hits faster and with less explanation. Surveys show that **64% of Gen Z workers fear losing their jobs in the next year[4]**, a higher percentage than any other generation. And this isn't just a feeling—entry-level layoffs have been particularly brutal. During the 2023 tech-sector contractions, younger hires were often the first to be let go[5]. Many Gen Z workers, barely a year into their first job, received notice via email that their corporate accounts were deactivated. Some reported finding out only after they were locked out of work laptops and Slack channels. The abruptness left them not just unemployed, but blindsided—a stark reminder that job loss today can arrive with the cold efficiency of an automated system. Where Gen X feared long gaps in employment, Gen Z fears the sudden shock of being digitally "locked out" of their accounts and cut off without warning.

Entrepreneurship and Business Failure

Both generations have flirted with entrepreneurship, but under very different conditions. Gen X learned that the American dream of small business ownership came with harsh odds. Many of us, myself included, discovered that self-reliance didn't guarantee success when market forces and human nature collided.

Gen Z has inherited that same entrepreneurial itch but faces even steeper challenges. High student debt, rising interest rates, and volatile digital markets make startups riskier than ever. A 2023 survey found that while **62% of Gen Zers express interest in starting their own business, fewer than 10% have launched one[6]**—and among those who do, failure rates mirror or exceed historical averages. Consider the wave of Gen Z–led online retail startups that boomed during the pandemic—Etsy shops, drop shipping businesses, and influencer-branded product lines. Many folded within two years, unable to keep up with rising costs, supply chain delays, or fierce competition. Like my coffee shop, they showed how enthusiasm and hard work aren't always enough to overcome structural odds.

Divorce and Relationships

Divorce was part of Gen X's cultural fabric. By midlife, **nearly half of Gen X marriages ended in divorce[7]**, making instability in family life an everyday reality. For many of us, the collapse of marriage felt almost inevitable—

we had grown up in homes where divorce was rampant in the '70s and '80s, and we often repeated those patterns.

Gen Z faces a different relational landscape. They are marrying later—or not at all. Marriage rates for adults under 30 have dropped to historic lows, which has kept their divorce rate lower for now[8]. But that doesn't mean Gen Z is insulated from rejection. Breakups, ghosting, and short-term relationships have become their version of divorce, with emotional fallout amplified by social media and the digital record of failed connections. In 2022, a Pew Research study noted that nearly **80% of young adults reported experiencing ghosting in dating[9]**. Unlike a private divorce, these rejections often unfold publicly—online posts disappearing, relationship statuses changing, or messages left unanswered. For many in Gen Z, heartbreak isn't hidden behind closed doors; it plays out on a stage where friends, acquaintances, and strangers can watch[10].

I've also watched my sons experience this new reality firsthand—how relationships form and dissolve online, often with a harshness that feels amplified. They've endured the cruelty of ghosting, the sting of social rejection, and the cultural attacks on masculinity that weigh on young men today. Add to that the rise of pornography and platforms like OnlyFans, which distort expectations of intimacy, and you see why mental health struggles among male adolescents are rising. For Gen Z men, rejection in relationships is not just personal but cultural, digital, and constant.

The Shared Thread

Despite their differences, both generations grapple with the same core truth: life will knock you down. The blows came slowly for Gen X—letters in the mail, meetings in conference rooms, divorce papers sliding across a table. The blows come instantly for Gen Z—a text message ending a relationship, an email auto-generated from a job portal, or a red balance in a startup account. Different delivery systems, same sting.

Generationally, both have also lived in the shadow of the groups that came before them. Gen X often felt eclipsed by the Baby Boomers, a generation born into postwar prosperity, strong unions, and a social order bent to their size and influence. We came of age in the hangover of that party—smaller in numbers, less politically catered to, and forced to adapt in leaner times.

Gen Z faces a similar dynamic, often standing in the long shadow of Millennials. For all their challenges, Millennials defined much of the cultural conversation over the last two decades: social media, the gig economy, and the shift toward activism in the workplace. Gen Z, by contrast, inherits the aftereffects—record student debt, inflated housing costs, and a job market where even advanced degrees don't guarantee stability. Where Millennials were often described as optimistic "digital natives," Gen Z wrestles with harsher realities: higher rates of anxiety and depression, constant online comparison, and an economy that feels less forgiving than ever.

And yet, here's where the parallels come into focus. Gen X and Gen Z must answer the same question: When rejection arrives—whether slowly or instantly—will it become a stopping point or a turning point? Gen X learned to wait, endure, and push through seasons of scarcity until opportunities reemerged. Gen Z must learn different skills: to filter the noise, recalibrate quickly, and protect their sense of identity in a world that never stops broadcasting success stories from everyone else.

The lesson, however, is universal. Failure doesn't define you unless you let it. Both generations, in their own ways, are being tested to see whether rejection will merely wound—or whether it will become the raw material of resilience.

Every generation gets knocked down. What matters most is not the fall, but the framework for getting back up. Here are four lessons I've learned—through my own failures, the stories of others, and the struggles of my own sons—that show how setbacks can become stepping stones.

1. Reframe Failure as Feedback

Rejection is not a verdict—it's information. Each "no" carries a message about what to adjust, refine, or improve. Instead of treating failure as final, treat it as data.

Take the example of J.K. Rowling. Her manuscript for *Harry Potter* was rejected by 12 publishers before it found a home[11]. Each rejection letter probably stung, but each one reinforced the need to keep pushing. What looked like failure was feedback that she hadn't yet found the right fit.

For me, this lesson came during my sophomore year of college. I sent out more than 50 queries for engineering internships one summer, hoping for a single "yes." I would have been ecstatic if my 13th attempt landed a position. But in 1986, we were still seven years away from the first working internet browser. Instead of searching online, I went to the library to look up prospective companies. Each application meant hours of research, manually typing letters, and walking them to the post office. What takes moments today took days back then. Over the next two months, rejection letters trickled in one by one.

With no internship, I returned to my summer camp counselor job during the day and picked up work in a little Cupertino restaurant called Pacific Steamer—known for pizza, steaks, and clams. It looked like failure on paper, but in reality, I was learning to cook for myself and developing some of my early parenting skills.

Skill for Today: When you don't get the internship, scholarship, or job, ask for feedback. Even a single insight —"We wanted more leadership experience"—can turn rejection into a roadmap for what to pursue next.

2. Separate Outcome from Identity

Failure in one area does not define your worth. Too often, we confuse what happened to us with who we are. That confusion magnifies rejection and makes it feel personal when it isn't.

As a sophomore, Michael Jordan was famously cut from his high school varsity basketball team[12]. The coach wasn't saying he was unworthy—only that he wasn't ready yet. Jordan used that sting to fuel relentless practice, proving that identity isn't bound to a single outcome.

I think of my oldest son, Julian, in a similar way. After stepping away from football due to injury, he felt adrift. Unsure of what came next, he asked me to co-sign a loan for flight school. My saying "no" probably came as a surprise because I had always supported his athletic pursuits. But this was different—he needed to discover for himself what he was capable of, on his own, without dad's safety net. It was time to take the training wheels off.

And he did. Like Michael Jordan he got committed to proving himself. Julian scraped together $10,000 of his own money to pay for his private pilot's license. That decision wasn't just about flying but about taking ownership of his future. Rejection from one dream didn't define him; it redirected him.

Skill for Today: Remember that injuries, grades, making team cuts, job offers, or relationships are snapshots—not permanent verdicts. Separate the moment from the person you are becoming.

3. Build a Recovery Ritual

Resilience is not automatic. You have to create habits that help you process failure and reset. Recovery rituals—whether journaling, working out, taking a long walk, or leaning on a trusted friend—create the margin you need to regroup before trying again.

Being the space guy I am, I can't resist using the Apollo program as an example. After the tragic Apollo 1 fire in 1967—the year I was born—NASA didn't abandon the program. They paused, reflected, rebuilt, and then launched Apollo 7, the first successful crewed mission. That ritual of reflection and redesign became the foundation that made future missions safe and successful.

My middle son, Quinn, faced his own recovery effort during the COVID era. The isolation, compounded by social media pressures, triggered deep mental health struggles. When suicidal ideation appeared, his mom, his stepmom, and I did what any parents would—searched for help. Unfortunately, the conventional wisdom at the time was to medicate first and ask questions later. Within a month, Quinn was prescribed the maximum dosage for a minor on two separate drugs. A month later, after turning 18, he was overprescribed again. Like so many in his generation, he ran headlong into a system that relied heavily on antidepressants[13], despite growing evidence that overprescription can actually worsen the risk of suicidal thoughts in adolescents and young adults[14]. When those medications failed, new ones were added. At one point, my son had become a walking, drooling zombie, showing no signs of real improvement.

That's when I stopped paying for the treatment-by-pill strategy and enrolled him in Capstone, a program in rural Arkansas that approached mental health differently. Instead of numbing symptoms, it addressed the underlying traumas—the "steam in the kettle"—and taught strategies for releasing pressure in healthy ways. The program was faith-based, but not preachy, striking a balance that resonated with him.

Quinn came out stronger. He learned coping skills, found a healthier balance, and built resilience. Today, he works at Chick-fil-A, earning not only a paycheck but also an online degree funded by the company. His outlook is wise but straightforward: *"I may not know exactly what I want to do, but it will probably cost money. So, while I'm figuring it out, I'm making money for the day I do."* As a father, I couldn't be prouder of how he built his own recovery plan and how he sticks to it today.

Skill for Today: Create your own rituals. Journal daily setbacks, reframe them into lessons, and physically reset with something grounding. Pausing is not weakness; it's preparation for the next attempt.

4. Leverage Rejection as Redirection

Sometimes the "no" you hear is the nudge you need toward the right path. Rejection can close doors that were never meant for you, forcing you to find the doors that are.

I grew up in Cupertino, across I-280 from the first Apple campus, and attended the same high school as Apple co-founder Steve Wozniak. The Apple name was everywhere in those days. That's why I remember vividly when Steve Jobs, the company's visionary, was fired in 1985[15]. The ousting of Apple's founder seemed incomprehensible to someone like me. But that rejection freed him to launch Pixar and NeXT, ventures that reshaped technology and entertainment. When Jobs returned to Apple years later, he brought the hard-earned experience that turned the company into a powerhouse.

My story of redirection came after my coffee shop business collapsed. At first, the pain blinded me to the lessons. But a few months after separating from my ex-wife, I was hired by a small defense company called USfalcon as an analyst for Training Systems Requirements Analysis (TSRAs). Initially, I wanted to remain a one-person deep subject matter expert, tucked away where I could be "the smartest guy in the room" and left alone to excel safely.

But necessity forced me forward. The government client needed more TSRAs; the only way to deliver was to build a team. Hiring others meant responsibility, and I feared repeating the cycle that had gotten me laid off in the first place. But instead of retreating, I leaned in. I built the ground floor, mastered the process, and hired the right people. Ironically, I found myself in the very position I had wanted in my restaurant—creating a system where others could succeed because I had laid the foundation. This time, I was ready.

Skill for Today: Understand that "no" often means "not yet" or "not here." Closed doors are sometimes the only way we find the right ones.

The Takeaway

Failure is not fatal, and rejection is not permanent. Reframe, separate, recover, and redirect. Learn from those who came before, but also write your own playbook (or process). Whether you're Gen X or Gen Z, the tools may differ, but the path is the same: get back up and keep going.

Failure and rejection sting—but they aren't the end of the story. They are the crucibles that shape character, sharpen skills, and prepare us for opportunities we can't yet see. Every generation learns this truth in its own way.

For Gen X, rejection came in paper envelopes, posted cut lists, layoffs, and divorce papers. We grew up knowing that not everyone makes the team, not every idea gets funded, and not every marriage lasts. For Gen Z, rejection often arrives instantly—an email shutting down your corporate account, a text ending a relationship, or silence after a job application disappears into the digital void. The pace and packaging are different, but the lesson is the same: you will get knocked down.

I've lived this personally—through layoffs, a failed business, and a broken marriage. I've watched my sons live it, too—through lost sports dreams, mental health battles, and the struggle to figure out who they are and what comes next. Every "no" hurts. But every "no" also pointed to the next step.

The takeaway is simple but powerful:

· Reframe failure as feedback.

· Separate outcomes from identity.

· Build recovery rituals that keep you grounded.

· Let rejection redirect you toward better paths.

These aren't abstract principles; they're practical survival skills. And they're yours to practice every day.

So, here's the challenge: the next time you hear "no"—from a boss, a college, a relationship, or life itself—don't let it stop you. Treat it as data, not destiny. Write down what you learned, reset your footing, and take the next step forward.

Because the real story of your life won't be written by the times you fell. It will be written by how many times you stood back up.

---

[1] Pew Research Center. *How the Great Recession Has Changed Life in America.* Pew Social & Demographic Trends, 2010.

[2] U.S. Bureau of Labor Statistics. *Entrepreneurship and the U.S. Economy*. Business Employment Dynamics.

[3] Bureau of Labor Statistics. *Patterns of marriage and divorce from ages 15 to 55: evidence from the NLSY79.* Monthly Labor Review, 2024.

[4] Newsweek. *Gen Z Living in Fear of Layoffs*. February 2024.

[5] CNBC. *Laid off by email: Tech workers share abrupt layoff stories*. 2023.

[6] Intuit QuickBooks. *Gen Z and Entrepreneurship: The Next Generation of Small Business Owners*. 2023.

[7] Bureau of Labor Statistics. *Patterns of Marriage and Divorce from Ages 15 to 55*. Monthly Labor Review, 2024.

[8] U.S. Census Bureau. *Marriage and Divorce Rates*. 2022.

[9] Pew Research Center. *The Virtues and Downsides of Online Dating*. 2022.

[10] American Psychological Association. *Adolescent Mental Health and the Impact of Pornography & Social Media.* 2023.

[11] “J.K. Rowling’s pitch for *Harry Potter* was rejected by 12 different publishing houses before it was accepted by Bloomsbury.” — Business Insider. Business Insider

[12] “He was cut from his high school varsity basketball team during his sophomore year.” — Elephant Learning article summarizing Jordan’s early setbacks. elephantlearning.com

[13] Between 2016 and 2022, the number of adolescents and young adults with ≥ 1 dispensed antidepressant prescription increased by 46.1% …” — study by Chua et al. in 2024. PMC

[14] “Safe use of SSRIs in young adults: how strong is evidence … Pooled adverse event data … showed a higher risk of suicidal ideation or behavior … 4% vs 2% …” — FDA meta-analysis via Grunebaum et al. PMC

[15] “In 1985, Jobs was ousted from Apple after a power struggle with then-CEO John Sculley” — TechRadar article on NeXT and Jobs’ departure. TechRadar

Chapter 6: Critical Thinking in an Age of Misinformation

A deep dive into sharpening independent thought, questioning authority, and navigating misinformation in a world where truth competes with noise.

As my boys grew up, I constantly gave them an option: we can do this the hard way or the easy way—it's your choice. My first two sons almost always chose the easy way. Julian, my oldest, was motivated by the things he loved: access to a video game, a favorite TV show, and playing sports. All I had to do was threaten to take one of those things away, and he quickly adjusted. Quinn, my middle son, tried to outsmart me early on. He claimed broccoli was his motivation at five years old, hoping I'd threaten to take it away. I gave him full credit for learning my parenting strategy at a young age, but he eventually submitted. I thought I was a parenting genius—they should have written books about me.

Then Ian, my youngest, came along and taught me that I knew nothing about parenting. When given the choice between easy and hard, Ian almost always chose hard. At age six, he started swearing, and the punishment was to have his mouth washed out with soap. One night, I had him bite into a bar of soap. After thirty seconds, I told him the punishment was over, and he could spit it out. In pure defiance, Ian looked at me and said, "No." He kept that soap in his mouth for another ten minutes, determined to show that he—not me

—would decide when it was over. In that moment, I realized I wasn't the master parent-jedi I thought I was.

What does this have to do with critical thinking? As someone with a doctorate in Education, I know the difference between behavioral learning, adjusting behavior to avoid consequences (touching the stove and learning what hot means), and cognitive learning, analyzing information and applying it to solve problems. [Note: For those who didn't know, cognitive learning is uniquely human—no animal, not dolphins, dogs, or apes, can do it.] When I told my kids they could choose the hard way or the easy way, I was really offering a choice between learning behaviorally or cognitively. Do it your way, face the consequences, or adopt what I already know to avoid unnecessary pain.

That's the essence of critical thinking: sifting through information to find the best approach before you "touch the stove." And in today's world, the stove is everywhere. Information bombards us nonstop—news alerts, TikToks, AI-generated videos, influencers with agendas. Some of it is true, some is half-true, and some is designed to mislead. The problem isn't finding information anymore; it's figuring out what's worth trusting.

For Gen X, the struggle looked different. We didn't have infinite feeds—we had three TV channels, a local paper, and a few radio stations. If you wanted to dig deeper, you had to put in real effort. More often than not, we chose to experience things rather than listen to guidance. We learned by trial, error, and sometimes pain. To be fair, our parents tried to warn us, but most of us figured it was more exciting to see for ourselves. That was our version of "touching the stove." Gen Z doesn't have to make that same choice. With massive access to information—and now tools like AI—you can learn cognitively rather than painfully, if you know how to filter truth from noise.

Today, the stakes are higher because misinformation spreads faster than ever. A rumor can circle the globe in minutes before the truth even has a chance to catch up. But the core skill—the ability to pause, question, verify, and think independently—is the same one that eventually carried Gen X through our own storms of mistrust.

This chapter is about that skill: critical thinking. It's about developing a mindset that doesn't blindly accept headlines, doesn't fall for the first viral post, and doesn't let someone else think for you. In an age of misinformation, critical thinking isn't just helpful. It's survival.

Because, in the end, life will always offer you two choices: you can touch the stove and learn the hard way, or you can think first and avoid getting burned.

For Gen X, the world of information looked nothing like it does today. We grew up just as cable television emerged. Before that, news meant 30 minutes of local coverage followed by a 30-minute national broadcast. Strip out commercials, weather, sports, and the human-interest closer, and you are left with 12 to 15 minutes of actual headline news each night. There were no 24-hour news channels until CNN launched in 1980.

If you were considered a "news junkie," you got your fix from the paper or a magazine. The New York Times, the Wall Street Journal, and USA Today set the national tone, while Time, Newsweek, and U.S. News & World Report shaped public opinion weekly. Today, those same outlets are mere fragments of what they once were, casualties of their failure to adapt to the digital age.

There also wasn't an involuntary bombardment of headlines coming into your life. No one rang your landline to drop a political agenda on you. Mostly, people got their news from sources they trusted, or from deep conversations in person. Our parents and grandparents were further removed—they passed information around barbershops, diners, or courthouse steps. That was their newsfeed. In college, doing research meant pulling dusty encyclopedias off the shelves or scrolling microfilm until your eyes crossed. In other words, information was scarce, and getting to it required effort.

That scarcity had an unexpected upside: it stood out when something didn't add up. When Walter Cronkite told the American people that the Vietnam War was unwinnable or when the Watergate scandal broke wide open, it shattered the assumption that authority figures and the media could be trusted without question. We learned that those in power—whether politicians, corporations, or journalists—weren't always telling the whole story.

That instinct to question authority became part of our DNA. You could hear it in the music we blasted and the culture we embraced. Punk rock wasn't just noise; it was defiance against being spoon-fed a version of reality we didn't buy. Underground zines (or the analog version of independent blogs or Reddit threads) circulated in dorm rooms and coffee shops, carrying voices you wouldn't find in mainstream print. Even TV reflected this ethos—*The X-Files* perfectly captured the Gen X mood: "Trust no one."

And yet, for all our skepticism, we lacked the tools to do much with it. Without alternative sources or real-time fact-checking, most of us still learned the hard way—by experience. Our parents warned us, but we often chose to test the boundaries ourselves, touching the stove and taking the burn. That balance—skeptical minds paired with limited information—defined the Gen X perspective. We learned not to take things at face value, but we also didn't have the wealth of resources Gen Z now holds in its pocket. In a strange way, that made us sharper. We developed a gut instinct for when something didn't feel right, even if we couldn't prove it.

Before going further, it's worth returning to the definition of critical thinking. In 1956, Benjamin Bloom and a group of educational psychologists created a framework for levels of intellectual behavior, known as *Bloom's Taxonomy[1]*. For the cognitive domain, the hierarchy runs from knowing something, to comprehending it, to applying it, to analyzing it, to evaluating it, and finally to synthesizing something new from it.

To put that in everyday terms—think about the game show *Jeopardy*. Contestants give the correct answer in the form of a question. It's a game built on who can recall the most names, dates, and terms. That's the lowest level of Bloom's taxonomy—Knowledge. We often assume winners of *Jeopardy* are brilliant, but in reality, they excel at memorization and recall. There's no deeper analysis, evaluation, or synthesis in play.

Critical thinking, by contrast, sits at the highest level of understanding. The Oxford definition describes it as "the objective analysis and evaluation of an issue in order to form a judgment." In short, it's the ability to take what you know, scrutinize it, and create new understanding. That's much harder than it sounds.

I saw this play out firsthand when I was finishing my doctoral dissertation. The primary purpose of a dissertation is for a doctoral candidate to demonstrate critical thinking. As one professor succinctly put it, the goal is "to add knowledge to the world." I saw colleagues who could recite definitions, quote theories, and reference thousands of sources—but when pressed, they couldn't tell me anything original about their subject, nothing that wasn't already written down somewhere. They knew, but they didn't think.

That's the key point I want you to hold onto as we move through this chapter: critical thinking isn't about how much you know. It's about what you can derive from the information you already have. That scrutiny often entails challenging something you believed to be true. That distinction—between gathering facts and creating understanding—will determine whether you fall for misinformation or rise above it.

I spend some time on IFunny. I'm always amazed at the broad spectrum of postings and memes—from jokes to politics to people venting their opinions. It's also a window into what people care about. My favorite are the posts that try to be data-driven: someone drops a chart, cites a legitimate source, then adds a comment as if to say, *"See, the numbers prove my point—how could you not agree?"* The problem is that's not critical thinking. That's knowledge at best, maybe comprehension. What's missing is the analysis, evaluation, and synthesis that lead to true problem solving.

Take housing, for example. I often see posts comparing household incomes and home prices from decades ago with today's numbers. The disparity is shocking and real. Homes are far less affordable now than when I bought my first house in 1994 in Warner Robins, GA. I paid $92,000 and used a VA loan at about 8.3% (Note: our rates were higher than today). With taxes and insurance, my payment was about $850/month. My monthly salary with housing and subsistence allowances was about $3,050, which put my debt-to-income ratio at 28%—a safe number by banking standards.

Fast forward to today. With a median home price of $410,000 and the average 20-something earning about $41,000 a year ($3,416/month before taxes), even a 20% down payment leaves you with a mortgage and escrow of about $2,800/month at a 7% rate. That's an 82% debt-to-income ratio. No lender in the country will touch that. So yes, the data proves the point—most Gen Zers are locked out of the housing market. But again, *so what?* Knowing homes are unaffordable doesn't tell you how to get one. Critical thinking is what takes you from *knowing* the situation to *solving* it.

And that's where the generational comparison comes in.

On the surface, Gen X and Gen Z seem worlds apart. One grew up on mixtapes, landlines, and waiting a week for the next episode of a show. The other has Spotify, iPhones, and entire seasons ready to binge in a single weekend. But when it comes to critical thinking and problem solving, the two generations share more than you'd think.

Similarities:

Both generations grew up distrusting "official stories." Gen X's skepticism came from watching institutions stumble—Vietnam, Watergate, corporate scandals, and shifting Cold

War narratives. For Gen Z, it comes from watching corporations, politicians, and influencers manipulate algorithms, headlines, and platforms. Both groups share the instinct to ask: *What's the real story here, and how do I make sense of it for myself?* In both cases, mistrust fuels problem-solving—forcing people to dig deeper, test assumptions, and find answers.

Differences:

The difference lies in the environment. Gen X dealt with scarcity. We had so few information sources that it was apparent when something didn't add up, but proving it was harder. Problem-solving meant using gut sense or painful trial-and-error. Gen Z faces the opposite problem: abundance. You live in a flood of news alerts, viral posts, AI-generated content, and influencers. The challenge isn't finding information; it's filtering, verifying, and then figuring out what to do with it.

For Gen X, skepticism often grew out of subcultures—punk scenes, underground zines, indie bookstores, and word-of-mouth. We learned to solve problems by finding voices outside the mainstream and piecing things together. Gen Z's skepticism, meanwhile, shows up in memes, group chats, and TikTok stitches that poke holes in narratives. But too often, Gen Z is told only that "your situation sucks"—that housing is unaffordable, wages are stagnant, politics are broken—without being given the why behind it or the tools for building a realistic path forward. Knowledge without problem-solving leads to frustration, not progress.

Ultimately, both generations wrestle with the same core question: *Who can I trust?* For Gen X, the answer often came from cultivating a gut suspicion and learning by getting burned. For Gen Z, the answer will come from mastering verification—fact-checking, cross-referencing, and analyzing data in real time, then turning that into actionable plans.

That's the bridge between the two: Gen X sharpened the skill of questioning, and Gen Z has the tools to take questioning further, but success depends on turning questions into solutions.

Critical thinking sounds like an abstract skill, but it's a disciplined way of solving problems in practice. It's what separates knowing facts from using facts to make life better. Gen X learned this slowly, often by "touching the stove" and paying the price. Gen Z has the opportunity to learn it faster—by applying analysis and evaluation to the flood of information you already have.

So how do you do that?

1. Follow the cognitive ladder, not just the data.

Think back to Bloom's Taxonomy. Knowledge and comprehension are only the starting points. The real power comes from applying, analyzing, evaluating, and synthesizing. On IFunny, you'll see charts on housing affordability: wages vs. home prices then and now. The knowledge is solid, but without the higher levels of thinking, you're all left with frustration. The real work begins when you ask: *Why is this the case? What forces created it? What options do I have within my circumstances?* Posting a chart won't get you into your first house. Synthesizing a realistic plan—whether that means a side hustle, relocation, or a creative financing strategy—will.

2. Use the "easy way or hard way" framework.

When I raised my boys, I always told them: We can do this the easy way or the hard way. My oldest learned quickly that adjusting his behavior to keep what mattered to him was the "easy way." My youngest, Ian, almost always chose the hard way, even holding soap in his mouth for ten extra minutes to prove he was in control. That lesson applies here. In life, you can insist on learning everything by experience—touching the stove until you're burned—or you can take the easy way: apply the information already available to avoid unnecessary pain. Gen Z has access to unprecedented data and AI tools. The easy way is to think critically, filter the noise, and use what's already known to make better choices before the burn.

3. Filter, then evaluate.

Gen X learned to question authority because information was scarce. When the government or media got it wrong, it stood out. But proving it was harder. We often relied on gut instinct or trial and error. Gen Z has the opposite challenge: drowning in abundance. To solve problems today, you need a filter. Ask simple questions: *Who benefits if I believe this? Can I find a different perspective? What evidence supports or contradicts this claim?* Filtering is only the first step—evaluating what's left and synthesizing a way forward is the real goal.

4. Translate skepticism into solutions.

Both generations share the instinct to distrust official stories. Gen X was impacted by Vietnam, Watergate, and the Cold War. Gen Z lives through algorithm-driven news feeds, viral disinformation, and influencer manipulation. But skepticism alone isn't enough. If all you do is call out problems, you're no closer to solving them. The challenge is to take that instinct and channel it into practical solutions. Don't just sharpen the question; master the answer.

5. Apply critical thinking to your own life first.

The big issues—housing affordability, politics, climate—can feel overwhelming. But critical thinking starts small. Run the numbers on your own finances. Test your own assumptions about your career path. Evaluate the reliability of the people you follow online. Don't just repost a chart; ask what it means for you, in your situation, with your goals. That's where the skill turns from theory into survival.

Let's take the following **Case Study: Housing Affordability**

Knowledge: Home prices are much higher relative to wages than in 1994. That much is undeniable—you don't need to scroll long on IFunny or Instagram before finding charts that show the disparity.

Comprehension: This means housing is less affordable for young buyers today, and on the surface, it can feel like an impossible system stacked against you. Many believe it's the rich getting richer and everyone else being a victim. While that frustration is real, it doesn't explain *why* the system looks the way it does or help solve the problem.

Application: Compare your salary, debt, and savings to local housing costs. A $41,000 annual salary, a median U.S. home price over $400,000, and today's mortgage rates make the numbers bleak. However, application is where critical thinking begins—you must run your own numbers, not just repost someone else's chart.

Analysis: Break down the fundamental drivers. It isn't just "greed." Inflation pushes prices up, but what drives inflation? Fuel prices, government spending, rising minimum wages, and even local zoning and regulatory policies all contribute. These aren't abstract forces—they're political and economic decisions, many of which remain popular with voters. Understanding the causes helps you move past outrage to insight.

Evaluation: Once you know the causes, you can evaluate your options. The housing market in your area may be out of reach, but another region isn't. That was my own situation. I grew up in California, where housing was unaffordable even in the 1990s. But during a year in the Arctic, I banked nearly all of my salary by living off my TDY pay. When I transferred to Georgia—a much lower cost of living—I was ready to buy my first home. It wasn't glamorous, but it got me in the door of home ownership. Similarly, options today might include relocating, considering multigenerational housing, looking at rent-to-own arrangements, or using creative financing strategies.

Synthesis: Build a plan tailored to your situation that gets you closer to ownership rather than just posting memes about how bad it is. The synthesis step requires you to take what you know about macroeconomic forces, combine it with your personal data, and generate a realistic path forward. That might mean saving aggressively in one season of life to buy in another, or choosing location over convenience, or exploring assistance programs that align with your circumstances.

The bottom line: Critical thinking is problem-solving. It's not about memorizing facts or pointing out problems—it's about using information to create workable solutions. Gen X had to learn this through scarcity and pain. Gen Z can learn it through abundance and application. The question isn't whether you know the facts but whether you can turn them into action.

This past year, I bought my first investment property. I started planning more than five years ago when I saw a downturn coming. Yes, the economy hit the *technical* definition of a recession—two quarters of negative GDP. The administration, with plenty of media support, framed it as a "transition" and argued GDP was only one piece of a bigger puzzle. I didn't need to win that debate. After living through eight recessions, I recognized the pattern and acted.

I expected the Fed to raise rates—and it did. I expected housing to stall in many markets—and it did. Three years ago, I began setting money aside for the drop I believed would arrive. I told my wife the plan: buy when prices softened, lock in a lower condo price as the Fed neared a pivot, and be ready to refinance when rates eventually fell—timing unknown, preparation certain. Last year, I analyzed markets (with ChatGPT's help), looked for places where prices had spiked fastest, and identified a likely bubble. Florida fit: COVID-era demand sent tens of thousands of buyers south, pushing coastal prices to extremes. Then two hurricanes hit Tampa. Overextended owners sold at a loss. Their loss, my gain—not predatory, just disciplined problem solving built on years of lessons and today's AI tools. I researched nightly rates, occupancy, and operating costs and chose a turnkey property where the math worked.

That's the point: critical thinking isn't academic—it's a survival skill. Anyone can post a meme about how bad the economy looks. Not everyone can break the problem down, design a plan, and execute.

Gen X learned to question authority because we had to. We didn't have infinite feeds, and we learned by experience—sometimes by touching the stove and getting burned. Gen Z has something we didn't: abundant information and powerful tools to filter, verify, model scenarios, and act. You don't have to choose the hard way. Take history's lessons, combine them with the data at your fingertips, and chart a smarter course.

Stop treating yourself as a victim of broken systems and start operating as a problem solver. Housing, inflation, politics, and personal setbacks—none improve by *knowing* the facts alone. They improve when you ask more profound questions: **Why is this happening? What forces drive it? What can I realistically do now?** Then you move.

Your challenge: pick one problem in your life—big or small. Stop scrolling and complaining. Map it through the stages: **know → analyze → evaluate → synthesize → act.** Don't just *know* the problem—**solve** it.

Because in the end, life always gives you two options: touch the stove and learn the hard way, or think first, act wisely, and walk away unburned. **Always think for yourself, or someone else will think for you.**

---

[1] Bloom, B. S. (Ed.). (1956). *Taxonomy of educational objectives: The classification of educational goals. Handbook I: Cognitive domain.* New York: David McKay.

Chapter 7: Money, Debt, and the Illusion of Wealth

How to avoid financial traps, why credit cards and student loans aren't 'free money,' and the importance of long-term financial planning.

Money is one of the few things that can simultaneously feel like freedom and prison. For Gen Z, the paradox is even sharper—you're the most digitally connected, most marketed-to generation in history, and everywhere you turn, the message is the same: spend more, upgrade faster, look successful now.

When I was a sophomore in college at Oklahoma State, tuition was about $30-$40 per credit hour and roughly $1,000-$1,200 per year for a full-time, in-state undergraduate like me. The most significant costs for the average student were simple—gas at $0.93 a gallon, a large pizza for about $6, and a decent used car for around $3,800 with monthly payments of $70. The minimum wage was $3.35 an hour, so working part-time 25 hours a week after taxes netted about $325 per month. This ensured I still had enough left to buy beer, which was about $4 for a twelve-pack.

I make this point because it sets the stage for a story about one of my fraternity brothers, Sean. One day, as he walked near the student union, he came across an American Express rep sitting at a table. From that encounter, Sean walked away with a shiny new credit card and a $1,000 line of credit. That month was a blur of fun—for Sean and the rest of us—because he was buying rounds of beer, eating out, picking up new clothes, and enjoying the good life.

The problem was that Sean didn't realize American Express cards didn't allow minimum payments. The entire balance was due in full every month. Sean had no job and lived on a fixed allowance from his parents. When he got the bill for nearly a thousand dollars, he gasped. Almost an entire year's tuition. His only option was to negotiate a repayment plan—with a sky-high interest rate—and drop out of school to work full-time just to pay it off. It took him over a year to climb out of that hole.

You'd think watching Sean's crash-and-burn moment would have taught me the lesson. But like most young adults, I was still in my "touching the stove" phase. I'd eventually make my own mistakes with money and debt before I learned the hard lessons that allowed me, years later, to afford things like investment properties in Florida.

Here's the hard truth: much of what gets sold as "wealth" is just an illusion built on debt. Credit cards promise convenience but hide crushing interest rates. Student loans feel like an investment in the future, but can follow you for decades. Social media adds fuel to the fire, convincing people to live beyond their means in pursuit of likes and validation.

Why does this matter? Because money isn't just about possessions—it's about options. When you're buried in debt, your choices shrink. When you plan and invest early, your choices multiply. The challenge of this chapter isn't just about avoiding debt traps; it's about learning to see money for what it really is: a tool. Used wisely, it builds freedom. Used carelessly, it builds chains.

In this chapter, we'll cut through the myths and illusions around money. We'll look at how previous generations (including mine, Gen X) stumbled through these same traps, how your generation faces a new level of pressure, and most importantly, how you can break the cycle by focusing on long-term financial planning instead of short-term appearances.

For Gen X, money lessons often came the hard way. We grew up in a world where credit cards were aggressively marketed on every college campus, student loans were easier to get than ever, and the American Dream seemed tied to how quickly you could buy a car, a house, or the latest gadgets.

When I was in college, it wasn't unusual to see credit card reps handing out free T-shirts, Frisbees, or water bottles in exchange for filling out an application. Companies weren't shy—they knew young adults were a perfect target: little financial knowledge, no steady income, but plenty of desire to spend. I watched my fraternity brother Sean stumble badly with his first American Express card. Not long after, I had my own stumbles. Like many peers, I had to "touch the stove" before truly understanding the pain of carrying debt.

By the time I graduated from college, I had racked up about **$800 in credit card debt**. At an interest rate of 20%, that meant a **$30 minimum monthly payment**. I could manage the payment on my monthly salary of **$1,387**, but I wasn't making a dent in the balance. Then my car broke down, and the repair bill was $300. My cards were maxed out, so I had no way to cover it. Desperate, I went to a small-town bank near my duty station. Fortunately, the loan officer—seeing I was military with a steady job—took pity on me. He gave me a personal loan at a reasonable rate, structured it so that it consolidated my card balances, and laid out a plan to pay off all my debt in three years. Then, in a moment that burned into my memory, he slid a pair of scissors across the desk and made me cut up both cards right in front of him. I felt embarrassed, but also relieved. That man in Clovis, New Mexico, quite literally saved my financial future. Four years later, when I was stationed in Georgia and ready to buy my first home, his tough love made it possible.

For Gen X, the traps were everywhere:

· **Credit cards** with double-digit interest rates are marketed as "flexible spending" tools.

· **Student loans** that seemed manageable at first, but for many turned into years of repayment.

· **Car loans** that convinced us it was better to have a new vehicle with payments than a used one without.

· **The illusion of ownership**—a house, a stereo system, a shiny TV—all "financed" and technically owned by the bank.

At the time, it didn't feel unusual. Everyone seemed to be doing it. Debt was sold as normal, even smart: "leverage" was the buzzword, and "buy now, pay later" was the lifestyle. But the long-term consequences were very real. Carrying debt delayed our ability to save, invest, and build real wealth. Many of us spent the first decade of our adult lives digging out of holes we'd created in our twenties.

Here's the important comparison: in the mid-1980s, the **minimum wage was $3.35 an hour**. That sounds low today, but so were the costs—**tuition at a public university like Oklahoma State was about $1,100 per year**, the **average used car cost around $5,000**, and **gas was under a dollar a gallon**. Even the average student loan burden was small by today's standards—just a few thousand dollars, not tens of thousands. For many Gen Xers, a summer job could cover tuition, and part-time work during the school year could keep the lights on.

I remember friends who worked construction or waited tables all summer, and by the time fall rolled around, they had tuition paid and money in the bank for books and rent. Work-study jobs on campus—library shifts, dining hall gigs, even clerical work in professors' offices—were enough to keep a student afloat without borrowing. I worked restaurant jobs, usually between 20 and 30 hours a week. The pay helped, but the real advantage of food service was all the free meals—it saved me a fortune.

That's not the reality today. Even with steady part-time work, Gen Z students often can't cover a fraction of their tuition and living expenses without loans.

If there's one key lesson my generation had to learn, it's this: **debt is easy to get into and hard to get out of.** I was lucky to get tough-love advice early on. Faced with the inability to repair my car because I had maxed out both of my cards, I turned to that small bank in eastern New Mexico. Because I was in the military, they took a chance on me and, with some old-fashioned fatherly intervention, put me on a plan that paid off my debt and gave me a second chance. That intervention allowed me to eventually build wealth instead of staying stuck in debt—and only a few years later, I was in strong enough financial shape to buy my first home.

The stakes are even higher for Gen Z, making learning to see through the illusion of wealth more urgent than ever.

Every generation faces its own money traps, but the patterns rhyme. Gen X and Gen Z share more in common than you might think—yet the scale of today's challenges is far greater.

Similarities

Easy Credit

When I was in college, credit card companies were everywhere. They'd hand out Frisbees, water bottles, or T-shirts to get you to sign up. One of my fraternity brothers, Sean, learned the hard way when he picked up an American Express card at a table near the student union, ran up a quick $1,000, and then discovered the entire balance was due in 30 days. Not long after, I had my own brush with $800 of credit card debt at 20% interest. I wasn't sinking yet, but I was treading water, and one unexpected car repair nearly sent me under. A sympathetic loan officer in Clovis, New Mexico, bailed me out and forced me onto a repayment plan that became my first real financial education. For Gen Z, the method looks different—"buy now, pay later" apps, instant approvals, and one-click shopping—but the trap is the same: easy credit, hard consequences.

Cultural Pressure to Spend

Growing up Gen X meant constant cultural pressure to look like you had more than you did. In rural Oklahoma, where I spent part of my youth, money was scarce and even families like mine with a small business struggled. Yet we still measured ourselves against appearances—whether it was the new car, the mall shopping trips, or the MTV version of "cool." When I was with my dad and stepmother in Silicon Valley, the money pressure looked different: more income, but still a "don't talk about money" culture that left me without the tools to understand financial management. Gen Z faces that same tension on steroids. Instead of malls and catalogs, you scroll TikTok and Instagram, where curated lifestyles make it look like everyone else your age is already rich. The message hasn't changed—spend more, upgrade faster—but the volume has been cranked way up.

Learning the Hard Way

The hardest lesson came later, when I thought I was finally financially stable. I had a decent credit score, a working car, a savings account, and even a house. What I didn't have was preparation for the financial responsibility of marriage. During our Catholic engagement encounter weekend, my fiancée and I were asked how much we thought we could spend without telling the other. I wrote down $50. She wrote $500. The difference was laughed off then, but it foreshadowed years of trouble. Nineteen years later, during our divorce, I discovered she had quietly accumulated $35,000 of credit card debt on top of the $25,000 I already knew about. That $60,000 was enough to sink me, and at 47 years old, I had to declare bankruptcy. Gen X and Gen Z share this reality: debt is seductive going in and brutal coming out. Emergencies come when you least expect them, and the bill always arrives.

Differences

The Size of the Debt

In the 1980s, student loans were measured in the low thousands. Even for someone like me—splitting time between rural Oklahoma and the growing Silicon Valley—the idea of graduating with over $10,000 in debt was rare. Tuition at Oklahoma State was about $1,100 a year, and summer jobs plus part-time work could often cover it. Gen Z doesn't have that luxury. Today, $30,000–$40,000 in debt is common, and many walk across the stage with six-figure balances before they've earned a single paycheck. The stakes are higher, and the runway to financial stability is much shorter.

Housing Affordability

Fortunately, after my financial rescue in New Mexico and a few years of discipline, I could buy my first home in Georgia. Starter homes were affordable on a modest salary, even with a military paycheck. For Gen Z, purchasing a first home feels out of reach. Prices have soared, mortgage rates are higher and saving for a down payment while paying off student loans and covering rent is nearly impossible. What was once a rite of passage for Gen X is now a distant dream for many Gen Z adults.

Wages vs. Costs

When I was young, friends worked construction or waited tables all summer, often covering a year's tuition and books. I worked restaurant jobs myself, usually 20–30 hours a week. The wages helped, but the real savings came from free meals, which saved me a fortune in food costs. Gen Z doesn't have that option. Even with the same hours, today's students can't come close to covering tuition or living expenses. Wages haven't kept pace, while tuition, housing, insurance, and healthcare have skyrocketed. The math doesn't work.

Social Media Pressure

Gen X compared ourselves to neighbors down the street or co-workers in the office. The pressure was local and, at times, manageable. Gen Z lives under a microscope of global comparison. Every scroll on TikTok or Instagram brings another image of a peer—or influencer pretending to be a peer—living a life of luxury. Sometimes it's rented cars or borrowed clothes, but the illusion is convincing. For Gen X, the illusion of wealth came from malls and catalogs. For Gen Z, it's delivered directly into your pocket 24/7. The pressure is louder, constant, and far more deceptive.

The Bottom Line

Both generations wrestle with the illusion of wealth, but the scale has shifted. For Gen X, the traps were credit cards, car loans, and the belief that "buy now, pay later" was a smart strategy. For Gen Z, the traps are student loans, inflated housing, digital debt schemes, and the nonstop pressure of social media.

I've lived on both sides. I learned some lessons the hard way—cutting up my credit cards in front of a loan officer, watching a marriage collapse under hidden debt, and even declaring bankruptcy in midlife. But I've also lived the other side: remarrying a financially wise woman, building a disciplined savings plan, paying for vacations and dinners in cash, and investing 15% of every paycheck. The security and freedom I feel today—four years from paying off my mortgage and on track for retirement—is unlike anything I experienced in the first four decades of my life.

The underlying truth hasn't changed: **real wealth isn't about appearances—it's about freedom of choice.** Gen Z will face bigger numbers, harsher conditions, and louder illusions, but the principle remains. If you can learn to spot the illusion early, resist the traps, and build real financial discipline, the freedom that comes with true wealth is still within reach.

History shows that downturns don't just destroy wealth—they also create opportunities for those who are ready. Take the **2008 housing crash** as an example. Home values across the

U.S. dropped by nearly 30%, and in some places like Las Vegas, Phoenix, and Florida, they fell by 50% or more[1]. For many families, it was devastating—foreclosures spiked, retirement accounts vanished, and credit markets locked up.

But not everyone lost. First-time buyers who had been priced out suddenly found homes within reach. Investors with cash or strong balance sheets bought foreclosures and short sales at deep discounts. Many of those properties had doubled or tripled in value a decade later. The difference between those who got crushed and those who got ahead came down to one thing: **preparation**.

That's the lesson for Gen Z. You don't know when the next downturn will hit—but you can be ready for it. Suppose you avoid the traps and build a savings and smart investing foundation. In that case, you'll be able to take advantage of tomorrow's buyers' markets instead of being sidelined by debt.

1. Understand the Illusion of Wealth

Wealth isn't the car you drive, the vacations you post online, or the brand name on your shoes. Those things might look good, but they often sit on a pile of debt. Real wealth is freedom—the ability to choose how you spend your time and money without a creditor deciding for you.

I say this as someone who fell for every illusion along the way. I bought into the credit card trap, carried balances, chased after things I couldn't afford, and believed the myth that debt was normal. It's human nature to fall for these things—every marketing agency knows that, which is why their advertising works so well. But I'm also proof that you can eventually learn, even if it takes time and hard lessons. If you didn't grow up with financial mentoring, take it upon yourself to learn the basics. There are plenty of free online courses that teach personal finance and economics. The knowledge is there—you have to decide if it matters.

2. Avoid the Debt Trap

· **Credit cards:** Use them as a tool, not as income. If you can't pay the balance in full monthly, you're living beyond your means.

· **Student loans:** Borrow the minimum necessary and have a payoff strategy before you sign the first promissory note.

· **Lifestyle creep:** Don't let every pay raise translate into more debt. Keep living below your means and invest the difference.

I was guilty of each of these traps. The lesson I eventually learned is simple: debt steals your freedom. If you want to be prepared for the next housing downturn—or any financial opportunity—you need to stay out of the hole so you're free to move when others can't.

3. Harness the Power of Compound Interest

Every dollar you save and invest early has decades to grow. The flip side is also true—every dollar you borrow can take decades to repay. Which side of the equation you live on makes all the difference.

Case Study: Debt vs. Investment

Let's compare two 25-year-olds, Alex and Jordan.

Alex's Path – The Debt Trap

· At 25, Alex built up $10,000 in credit card debt. With an average interest rate of 20%, that debt grows fast. If Alex only pays the minimum each month (about $250), it will take nearly 6 years to pay off—and cost over $7,000 in interest alone. By age 31, Alex was finally free of debt, but had not invested anything and had lost valuable time.

Jordan's Path – The Investment Advantage

· Instead of carrying credit card debt, Jordan sets aside just $200 a month into a basic investment account earning a 7% annual return (the long-term historical stock market average). By age 31, Jordan had invested about $14,400, but the account was worth nearly $18,000 thanks to compound growth. Jordan has no debt, a financial cushion, and a 6-year head start on building real wealth.

The Long Game

· If Jordan keeps up that $200/month investment until age 65, the account grows to over $500,000. Even if they start investing later at the same rate, Alex ends up with less than half that amount. The difference isn't luck—it's the power of time, discipline, and avoiding the debt trap.

Lesson: Every dollar you spend on interest is a dollar you don't get to invest in yourself.

4. Build a Financial Safety Net

· Create an emergency fund for 3–6 months of expenses. This will prevent you from reaching for credit when life happens.

· Buy insurance that protects against catastrophic loss—health, auto, renters or homeowners. Insurance isn't exciting, but neither is financial ruin.

I often hear Boomers tell Millennials and Gen Zers that the solution is as simple as skipping the $6 Starbucks coffee. That advice is half-right and half-wrong. No one is going to buy a house just by skipping lattes—but if you redirect $6 a day into savings, you're suddenly putting aside $180 a month. That adds up. The real lesson is this: don't dismiss small beginnings. For Gen Z, the goal is to start small and build toward bigger goals.

5. Automate Good Habits

· Pay yourself first by setting up automatic contributions to savings and retirement accounts.

· Track your spending. Use an app if you like; even a simple notebook can reveal where your money goes.

· Stick to a plan. Freedom comes not from spontaneous purchases but from the steady discipline of living within your means.

I started by putting away just $20 a month into an investment account run by a local broker. Adjusted for inflation, that's about $50 today. It wasn't much, but it got me started. Later, when I landed my first defense contracting job, I took full advantage of the 401(k) matching option—investing 6% of my paycheck, with the company matching half of that. That meant the equivalent of 9% of my pay went into retirement before I saw it. Over time, I raised my contributions every time I got a raise. No matter the size of the raise, a portion got added to my investment, and now it's about 15% of my paycheck. Here's the trick: I didn't feel the loss because I never got used to spending that money. It was like giving myself a hidden inheritance.

If you can automate your savings and live as though the money isn't there, you'll build wealth in the background without the daily temptation to spend it.

6. Reframe What Wealth Really Means

Wealth isn't about possessions; it's about peace of mind. When you have no credit card debt, money in the bank, and a plan for the future, you sleep better at night. And that security is worth more than any shiny purchase.

As my wife and I look toward retirement, we don't measure wealth in cars or square footage—we measure it in freedom. How many weeks can we spend in Mexico each year? How many dinners out do we want to enjoy each month? If one of us lost a job, we'd be fine—we wouldn't lose the house. As one credit card commercial used to say, that feeling is *priceless*.

Wealth is not about appearing rich. It's about being free.

The truth about money is simple but easy to forget: it can either be your greatest tool or your greatest trap. Debt feels like freedom in the short term, but steals your choices in the long term. Savings and investments feel slow and tedious, but over time, they create peace of mind and open doors you never thought possible.

I've lived on both sides. I carried debt, made mistakes, and even hit bankruptcy. But I also learned discipline, rebuilt my financial foundation, and now live where financial freedom—not creditors—guides my decisions. That journey proves that it's never too late to turn around.

And I see Gen Z learning the same lesson, sometimes even earlier than we did. I only have to look at my oldest two sons, Julian and Quinn, to see that they are already far ahead of where I was at their age. Julian saved $10,000 selling solar panels to pay for his private pilot's license—no lattes, no impulse splurges. When he landed his first flying job as an instructor in Greeley, I helped him look at apartments. What impressed me was how he insisted on staying within his budget, willing to sacrifice comfort now for long-term security. He still calls a couple of times a month to run things by me. I chose a different path than my parents regarding money conversations. Instead of avoiding the topic, I brought up money often—mistakes and all—so my sons could learn from what I did wrong. Recently, Julian told me about a conversation with a mentor in his commercial airline internship program. When asked what he'd done with the $500 monthly stipend, which must be returned if he doesn't complete his internship, Julian said he had parked all of it in CDs. Low return, yes, but secure, and if he chooses to go to another airline, he doesn't have to fear the impending debt; he returns the money and keeps the interest. The mentor was stunned—few 23-year-olds show that kind of financial maturity.

Quinn is also on the right path. In high school, he and his best friend Oliver discovered the stock market through an online trading game. For him, the lightbulb wasn't just "you can make money from money"—it was that you could do it without physical labor. That led to conversations between us about compound interest. We worked out that $20 a week invested at 8% would grow into $1 million in 56 years. Today at 21, Quinn has a real investment account—something I didn't start until I was 30—and he's studying finance in college. He's already applying discipline, not just theory. And while my youngest, Ian, is still finding his way with money, I'm not worried. The beauty of financial discipline is that anyone can learn it. It doesn't require a degree or advanced math—just patience, consistency, and the ability to delay gratification for long-term freedom.

That's the difference preparation makes. It's not about being lucky—it's about being ready.

Here's your challenge:

1. Write down every debt you currently owe—no hiding.

2. Choose one small habit you can redirect into savings (skip one subscription, pack lunch twice a week, cut back on Uber Eats). It doesn't have to be much—$6, $20, whatever you usually spend on discretionary comfort.

3. Put that money toward building your emergency fund or paying down your smallest debt first. Remember: you're not trying to buy a house yet—you're trying to pay off debt and build wealth. And wealth doesn't always mean cash. It could mean a certificate that earns you a raise, training that opens a new career path, or skills that expand your earning potential—whether that's becoming a pilot, a plumber, or something else that adds value to your portfolio.

4. Commit to one year. At the end, look back and measure the impact. Then decide if you can keep going. Eventually, the habit becomes so ingrained you won't notice the money you've redirected.

Do this, and you've already taken the first step toward freedom. Because when the next downturn comes—and it will—the question is: will you be scrambling to survive, or will you be positioned to thrive?

Looking back, I often think of Sean at the student union table, proudly flashing his new American Express card, and of myself a few years later, sitting across from a small-town loan officer in Clovis, New Mexico, cutting up my cards in embarrassment. Two very different moments shaped how I came to understand money. Sean's mistake showed me how easy it is to fall into the trap; my rescue showed me how powerful it is to climb out with discipline and guidance. Those lessons still echo today: debt is easy, freedom takes work, and your choices in your twenties can ripple for decades.

If you take anything from this chapter, let it be this—learn from our stumbles so you don't have to repeat them.

And remember: *Don't chase the illusion of wealth—build the reality of freedom.*

---

[1] Lincoln Institute of Land Policy, *What the Housing Crisis Means for State and Local Governments*, 2011. Available at: https://www.lincolninst.edu/publications/articles/what-housing-crisis-means-state-local-governments

Chapter 8: Work Ethic in a Changing Job Market

The difference between working hard and working smart, why 'quiet quitting' won't get you ahead, and how to build a career on value rather than entitlement.

The job market is shifting under our feet. Remote work, side hustles, automation, and AI are rewriting the rules faster than any generation has ever experienced. For Gen Z, entering the workforce means stepping into a world where old formulas—work hard, stay loyal, climb the ladder—don't always hold up. At the same time, new shortcuts like "quiet quitting" or coasting by on the bare minimum promise an easy path forward, but in reality, they lead nowhere.

I still remember my start in the working world and how much it shaped my understanding of work ethic. My very first paying job that involved a W-2 was with the fast-food chain Hardee's. Before that, I pulled water pumps out of wells for my stepfather and worked at a local skating rink, handing out rental skates for $2 an hour under the table plus free skating. When I turned 16, I couldn't wait to get that first "real" job and a steady paycheck.

In my small town of Tahlequah, Oklahoma, jobs weren't easy to come by. McDonald's and Wendy's weren't hiring, and most local businesses were family-owned. If you didn't have connections, you were out of luck. When a new Hardee's announced a grand opening and interviews, I jumped at the chance. Getting hired felt like winning the lottery. I was trained on the grill, helped open the store, made new friends, and discovered that work wasn't just about money but belonging. My paycheck went toward paying off my truck, putting gas in the tank, and the rest? It went to fun. That first job gave me more than spending money; it gave me independence.

A year later, when I moved to California to live with my dad, my top priority wasn't grades or making friends—it was getting another job. In my first week at school, I heard a girl mention that McDonald's down the street was hiring. I walked over that same afternoon and got hired on the spot. But this was a different world from Oklahoma. The service industry desperately needed workers in Cupertino, and turnover was constant. For many of my peers, jobs like this were optional. Their parents gave them generous allowances, and if they did work, they didn't take it seriously. What was the worst that could happen—getting fired?

They put me on the register on my first day at McDonald's. I had mastered the flat grill in Oklahoma, but this was something new. I learned quickly and thought I was doing fine—until the lunch rush hit. Suddenly, five registers were flooded with hundreds of customers. The manager announced a contest to motivate us: whoever took the most orders between noon and one would win a free lunch. I figured I didn't stand a chance as the new guy. But an hour later, to everyone's surprise, I won by a wide margin. Not because I was the fastest or the smartest—but because I cared about doing a good job. That effort alone set me apart.

Looking back, I realize how much those early jobs taught me. In Oklahoma, I was surrounded by people who worked hard because they had to. In California, where jobs were more plentiful, I saw the opposite—many treated work as disposable. Those experiences planted seeds that grew through the rest of my journey: high school, college, the Air Force, and later as a defense contractor and senior manager. The lesson was simple: work ethic matters. It doesn't guarantee everything, but it always creates opportunities. And just as important, you learn to spot who has it and who doesn't.

That's why I believe the truth about work ethic is as relevant now as it was then. It still matters—it always will. But it looks different today. It's not just about logging long hours or answering emails at midnight. It's about combining effort with strategy: knowing when to push, when to step back, and how to create real value in whatever role you're in.

This chapter explores that balance: the difference between working hard and working smart, why "quiet quitting" won't build you a future, and how to shift the question from *"What do I deserve?"* to *"What can I contribute?"* Because in the end, success doesn't come from entitlement—it comes from proving your worth in ways others can't ignore.

For many in Generation X, a strong work ethic wasn't optional—it was a requirement for survival. Many of us came of age during a period of economic turbulence that shaped our views on jobs, money, and opportunities. The early 1980s recession pushed U.S. unemployment above 10%, the highest level since the Great Depression[1]. By the time Gen X entered the workforce in the late 1980s and early 1990s, the national unemployment rate had dropped to around 5–6%[2]. Still, the scars of a "jobless recovery" lingered. Stable, lifelong employment was already on the decline. Layoffs, downsizing, and the shift to contract and service work taught us early that loyalty to a company didn't guarantee security.

That reality shaped how we worked. We were the latchkey kids who learned independence at a young age, and when we got our first jobs, we carried that toughness with us. For me, the difference between working in Oklahoma and California highlighted two truths about the Gen X experience. First, jobs weren't evenly distributed—rural communities often had more workers competing for fewer opportunities, while booming urban centers like Silicon Valley cycled through workers so fast that even a teenager could be hired on the spot. Second, the effort you put in mattered. At McDonald's in Cupertino, I quickly saw that many of my peers treated the job as expendable. I stood out simply by caring. That lesson carried forward: in a world where many coasted, showing up with effort and consistency opened doors.

However, I don't want to make it sound like everything in my generation was a kumbaya experience, where workers were always loyal and bosses were always fair. The balance of employee and owner had its issues. After three months at McDonald's, I became part of a tight-knit group of employees who thrived under the guidance of a great supervisor named Heidi. Together, we ran one of the strongest shifts in the store. We were so effective that when the owner needed a crew to cover his second location during a special event, we were the instant choice. That night we ran the store like a machine—sales were high, customers were happy, and everything seemed perfect. Except for one mistake: during closing, we didn't do a final sweep of the bathrooms. The place was spotless otherwise, but the next morning the opening crew discovered a masked robber had spent the night locked inside.

Whether he had been accidentally locked in by us or had intentionally planned to rob the store in the morning was never clear. But the fallout was swift: Heidi was blamed and terminated for failing to check the bathrooms. For our crew, it felt like betrayal. She was a great supervisor who had carried us to success, yet she was thrown under the bus for one oversight. In protest, we agreed to quit as a group. My condition was that I would give myself a couple of weeks to find a new job, which I did—at an independent pizza joint called Pacific Steamer just down the road. Ironically, I turned out to be the only one who followed through on our "mass walkout." Word of our planned revolt spread, and management eventually terminated everyone else in the group, one by one, for cause. I learned a tough but valuable lesson: loyalty matters, but workplace revolts rarely end the way you think.

Gen X as a whole leaned into that reality. We grew up learning that hard work builds trust and reputation, but also that institutions wouldn't always protect you. Surveys from the 1990s consistently showed that we valued work ethic as a defining trait—nearly 70% of Gen Xers in a 1993 Gallup poll said they believed "success comes from hard work, not luck."[3] At the same time, we weren't naïve. We watched Boomers give decades to one company only to be laid off, and we swore we wouldn't make the same mistake. That's why Gen X became known as both hardworking and skeptical. We proved ourselves through effort, but we also sought backup plans, such as side hustles, additional schooling, or developing skills outside of our job.

The data backs this up. In 1990, the median wage for workers under 25—the age when most of Gen X was starting out—was approximately $5.15 per hour, equivalent to roughly $11 in today's dollars. It wasn't much, especially with rising housing and education costs. By the time many of us reached our late 20s, student loan debt had tripled compared to Baby Boomers at the same age, and buying a home required far more income than it had a generation earlier. We were expected to "work harder for less"—and most of us did.

Still, that grind shaped us. We became adaptable, pragmatic, and resourceful. We didn't have the luxury of "quiet quitting"—if you didn't show effort, someone else would gladly take your spot. The lesson we carried forward is simple: hard work may not guarantee success, but lack of effort almost guarantees failure.

At first glance, Gen X and Gen Z don’t seem to have much in common. Gen X grew up largely independent—latchkey kids who learned self-reliance while juggling chores, part-time jobs, and limited resources. Gen Z, by contrast, has grown up hyperconnected, with information and opportunity a click away. However, it is where the two generations truly meet that they share a common response to disruption. Both entered the workforce in unstable times, forced to adapt quickly to survive.

I saw this in my own story, initially, with low-paying fast food jobs. While still in high school, I had already figured out one thing: if you didn't push beyond the bare minimum, you weren't going to stand out. Fast food jobs tend to be very simple and repetitive. I could have coasted—but instead, I spent my breaks learning about other people's jobs, asking questions, and building trust with the managers and owners above me. That extra effort paid off. When opportunity appeared, I was ready. I didn't always get that opportunity because I was the most talented. I got it because I showed initiative and trustworthiness—two traits that never go out of style.

And this is where Gen X and Gen Z diverge most sharply. Gen X, for all its skepticism, usually defaulted to "grind mode"—long hours, loyalty to bosses (sometimes misplaced), and a willingness to pay dues. Gen Z, on the other hand, is less willing to play that game. They question the point of grinding, and many embrace "quiet quitting," doing only what's required without giving more. To them, it feels like setting boundaries. To employers, it feels like coasting. That disconnect is widening a gap in how the two generations view work ethic, trust, and value.

Similarities. Both generations grew up in times of disruption. Gen X entered the workforce in the shadow of recessions, layoffs, and the dismantling of the promise of lifelong corporate employment. Gen Z is entering the workforce against a backdrop of automation, remote work, climate anxiety, and crises in housing and debt. Both generations learned early that the ground could shift quickly. As a result, they had to develop resilience and adaptability. Neither generation has the luxury of assuming stability is guaranteed.

Differences. Where Gen X leaned toward skepticism and survival, Gen Z leans toward flexibility and balance. Gen X often defaulted to the grind—working long hours, proving loyalty, and hedging with side hustles or extra education. Gen Z, on the other hand, has shown less tolerance for "just putting your head down." They're quicker to question why a job matters, what the return is, and whether the employer deserves their effort. In some ways, this is a positive development: Gen Z is less likely to sacrifice personal well-being for work. But it can also be misinterpreted as entitlement or laziness—especially by older Gen X managers who see echoes of their own struggles in a harsher economic climate.

Quiet Quitting. This is one of the clearest dividing lines. Quiet quitting isn't actually quitting—it's a mindset where workers decide to do only what's strictly required, nothing more. Gen Z often views it as a form of boundary-setting or self-preservation —a way to protect their mental health and avoid exploitation. However, from the perspective of managers and business owners, it appears as disengagement. In fact, a 2024 Morning Consult survey found only **36% of Gen Z workers considered themselves "very engaged" at work—13 points lower than the U.S. average[4]**. Gen Zers were also more likely than average to engage in quiet quitting behaviors, such as logging off early or sticking rigidly to the bare minimum.

I learned early on that initiative and trustworthiness can set you apart from the crowd. After my short stint at McDonald's, I was hired by a small pizza restaurant called Pacific Steamer. They also served steaks and clams, and I started as the pizza oven guy. The large rotating gas oven had three shelves, and on my first day, I dropped a couple of pizzas. Over time, I mastered the skill and began to pay attention to the hierarchy of jobs. The top spot was closing cook on Friday and Saturday nights—trusted to manage the store and close out on their own. I didn't set out to get that job, but during my breaks, I asked to learn grill skills. I picked up knowledge and gained the trust of Wanda, one of the owners, who had no patience for slackers.

Three months in, I got called in by the store manager, Scott, on a Saturday morning: "Can you come in and learn the closing grill job tonight?" I said yes. Overnight, I jumped three positions and got a 30% raise. The reason was simple: Wanda had caught the three closing cooks throwing a party in the store the night before. I, as the only person who had taken the initiative to learn any skills beyond their own, became the next in line; plus I had the trust of the owners. In today's quiet quitting environment, those two traits—initiative and trustworthiness—are often forgotten.

The danger for Gen Z is believing that employers owe them something beyond the paycheck. Poor treatment is always a valid reason to leave, but the idea that just showing up entitles you to more is a dead end. Businesses can only survive if they're profitable. I learned this painfully as a small business owner—when employees believed they were owed more than they were producing, the business collapsed, and their jobs disappeared overnight.

Hiring realities today. This shift isn't theoretical—it shows up in the hiring process. As a manager, I rarely take risks on brand-new grads. I check how many jobs someone has held in the past 5–10 years, and I review their social media presence. Too often, I find posts complaining about employers or demanding that companies change their practices to better suit employees. Whether or not their point has merit, my takeaway is simple: *this person lacks initiative and loyalty.* They're showing me they'd rather criticize than prove their value. That makes it easy to exclude their resume from the pile.

And this is where data supports the concern. A 2023 ResumeLab survey found **83% of Gen Z workers openly consider themselves job-hoppers[5]**. Job mobility can be healthy when it's about growth, but frequent movement without proving value raises red flags for employers who prize stability and commitment.

The lesson is simple. Gen Zers need to take responsibility for their own work ethic. Once hired, they should take initiative to build skills and add value—without demanding immediate pay raises. This costs nothing and requires no degree. Initiative and trustworthiness are free, but they're priceless in shaping a reputation.

I didn't fully understand the power of those traits until later in life—after I failed as a small business owner and returned to the defense industry. I accepted a job at a lower salary than before, grateful just to have a job. I proved myself day after day, without holding my value over the company's head. When the client recognized my contributions and my value skyrocketed, I showed loyalty to the company instead of leveraging for more pay. My philosophy was simple: *a rising tide lifts all boats.* If I focused on creating that rising tide, everyone, including me, would benefit.

The takeaway for Gen Z is clear: technology and times may change but work ethic doesn't. Initiative and trustworthiness will always separate those who move ahead from those who stay stuck.

Work ethic is not just about showing up—it's about how you show up, how you carry yourself, and how you prove your value over time. Gen Z faces a different job market than Gen X ever did, but the fundamentals remain the same. Effort and attitude still separate those who get noticed from those who get overlooked. The difference is that today you have to combine *hard work* with *smart work* if you want to move forward.

1. Understand the balance between working hard and working smart

Hard work builds discipline, but smart work multiplies your results. At Pacific Steamer, I didn't just sling pizzas. I paid attention to how the grill worked, watched the top cooks, and learned on my own time. That same lesson carried into my defense contracting career. I started out in business development but soon discovered I had a knack for systems engineering. Using my subject matter expertise as a space operator, I was asked to help craft a technical solution for a billion-dollar missile defense program. Our team won the contract, and from that experience, I picked up the ability to draft technical solutions for government proposals—skills that would pay off again later in my career.

That's the power of working smart on top of working hard. Gen Z can apply the same approach: don't just complete the task in front of you, but also learn about the job you want next. Seek out opportunities to expand your knowledge beyond your current area of expertise. The payoff is often greater than you realize.

2. Don't fall for the myth of quiet quitting

Quiet quitting may feel like self-preservation, but it's a reputation killer. Doing the bare minimum doesn't just limit your growth; it also forces teammates to pick up the slack. Managers and hiring leaders notice that. As a small business owner, I saw firsthand that when employees coast, the business suffers—and eventually, so do their jobs.

Quiet quitting also makes you less competitive. During that time of silent revolt, you're often cheating yourself out of growth. The months you spend disengaged could have been used to learn a new skill, gain industry insight, or build your network. You may think you're sending a message to your boss, but meanwhile, your coworkers are getting a leg up on you in value and opportunity. Quiet quitting doesn't hurt the employer nearly as much as it hurts the employee.

3. Build value before you expect reward

One of the biggest misconceptions in today's workforce is that employers owe you something beyond the paycheck. Some even argue they are owed a "livable wage," but the reality is that you are only owed what your work produces in value. That value isn't defined by you; it's defined by the market and the people taking the risk of running the business. If you depend on someone else for a paycheck, they will decide what you're worth. That doesn't mean you shouldn't seek higher pay elsewhere when your value isn't recognized —it means entitlement is not a strategy.

I've seen this play out in the defense industry. After eleven years of active duty, I joined the reserves and started working as a defense contractor. While on reserve duty, I often advised fellow service members who were leaving the military and explained the realities of the job market. Unlike the military, where you give six months' notice, most companies won't hire six months out—or even three. The sweet spot is often two to six weeks before your start date. That gap feels uncomfortable when you have a family asking where the household goods will be shipped, but it's a reality. Additionally, many job offers are contingent upon contracts being awarded. That means delays or cancellations can leave you stranded.

My advice has always been: take the first funded job you can get. Even if the pay is less than you hoped, you need a paycheck. Then commit to staying at least two years. Learn your job, but also learn the jobs of those around you. That extra layer of knowledge has gotten me—and others I've advised—opportunities we never expected. After two years, you gain leverage. You can be more selective and hold the power, as companies are often more desperate to fill roles quickly when they win contracts or lose key talent. But you must be careful not to chase paychecks blindly. I saw a young veteran jump ship for a 20% raise at a company in its last year of a contract. A year later, the company lost the work, and he was back at square one, unemployed. That lesson applies not just to military members transitioning out, but also to college grads and anyone entering the job market: build value first, then leverage it wisely.

4. Protect your reputation—online and offline

Hiring managers are watching more closely than ever. We examine the number of jobs someone has held in the past decade, and we thoroughly review their social media presence. Posting complaints about how employers "should" change may win likes from peers, but to hiring managers, it screams risk. We're asking ourselves, "Do I want to hire someone who spends time criticizing employers, or someone who demonstrates initiative and loyalty?" The answer is easy.

Protecting your reputation also means surrounding yourself with truth-tellers, not cheerleaders. I learned this during my first divorce. My first lawyer told me what I wanted to hear and racked up billable hours fighting pointless battles. My second lawyer gave me the hard truth: "This is where you'll lose, this is where you can win, and this is where to focus your fight." That blunt honesty saved me time, money, and sanity. In your career, you need the same reality check. Don't seek validation—seek truth, even when it stings. It's what helps you grow and make more intelligent choices.

5. Take Initiative to develop yourself—for free

The most crucial career builders don't cost money. Initiative, reliability, and trustworthiness are traits anyone can practice. They can't be bought, but they are noticed. Gen Z has endless access to information, but the ones who stand out are those who take responsibility to learn, practice, and add value without waiting for someone to assign it.

I see this in my youngest son, Ian. Born with the umbilical cord around his neck, he has a learning disability that makes memorization and comprehension difficult. He often has to work three times harder than others to grasp basic tasks. But that struggle built resilience. His greatest strength is not a skill you can put on a resume—it's his persistence, his willingness to stick with a task until it's done. That resilience, more than any degree or credential, is what will carry him forward in work and life.

The lessons are straightforward:

· **Don't confuse balance with coasting.** A healthy work-life balance is essential; disengagement is not. At Pacific Steamer, balance meant learning and growing even on breaks while working at minimum wage—it didn't mean refusing to grow because the job wasn't perfect.

· **Don't confuse value with entitlement.** Employers don't owe you beyond the paycheck your work earns. Value is created, not demanded. I've seen careers stall because people believed they were owed more than they produced.

· **Don’t confuse self-protection with disengagement.** Boundaries are healthy, but quiet quitting isn’t boundary-setting—it’s pulling back your own growth. When you stop investing in yourself, you’re not protecting yourself; you’re weakening yourself.

Ultimately, your work ethic is about being the person others can count on—not just today, but when it matters most. Initiative, trustworthiness, and resilience will always be the key to a competitive edge.

The job market will continue to shift—sometimes suddenly, sometimes in ways we don't expect. New technologies, industries, and workplace trends will emerge and evolve. But work ethic is timeless. It adapts, it evolves, but it never disappears. The person who can be counted on to take initiative, follow through, and add value will always rise above the noise.

Success today isn't about burning out, sacrificing your health, or living at the office. However, it's also not about coasting, quietly quitting, or expecting rewards simply for showing up. Real success lies in finding the balance point where effort meets value—where you bring energy, reliability, and creativity to your work in a way that others can see and depend on.

That's the advice I've given countless times to military members transitioning to the civilian workforce. Don't waste time looking for the job people tell you that you *deserve*, or the salary you think you can command—not at first. Get your foot in the door and start building your resume on day one. Take the job that is real, funded, and ready to put you on payroll. Then, once you're in, prove yourself. Don't jump ship at the first offer of a raise somewhere else. Learn your craft, become an expert in your field, and build a reputation that makes you indispensable. That's how you build leverage that lasts.

I've lived that lesson myself. When I was laid off from the defense industry in 2013, it felt like being sent back to the end of a thirty-year-long line. At forty-six, I didn't want to start over at the bottom, so I tried to carve out my own path. That venture ended in failure, but it gave me a new perspective—what it was like to be the boss, to carry the risk, to see firsthand what it takes to keep a company alive. That perspective made me a better fit when I returned to a small defense company.

After a decade of loyal, steady work there, I wasn't chasing promotions or titles. I wanted to do my job well enough that others who relied on me could do theirs securely. My loyalty was noticed. When Corporate posted a director-level role to oversee all Colorado operations, I didn't even apply. I was content running projects. But when the COO called and asked if I would step in as an interim solution, I said yes—not because I wanted the title, but because I wanted to protect the culture and projects I cared about. Eventually, the role became permanent, not because I "moved up," but because I helped create an environment where others could lead without interference.

I took a page from Scott Adams, the creator of *Dilbert*, who once described the best managers as the ones who remove obstacles from their team's path. That became my philosophy. My work ethic, drafted as a teenager in high school jobs, sharpened as an Air Force officer, tested as a defense contractor, and stretched as a small business owner, eventually matured into something bigger than my own career: a culture where others could thrive.

That's what work ethic really means. It's not about a job title or a salary. It's about consistency, persistence, and the willingness to create value for others. Over time, it builds trust. And trust builds opportunity.

So, here's my challenge to Gen Z: don't just ask, *"What do I deserve?"* Ask, *"What value can I create?"* Every opportunity, every job, every career step opens up when you answer that question honestly and put the answer into action.

---

[1] U.S. Bureau of Labor Statistics, *Unemployment Rate Reaches Postwar High in 1982, Monthly Labor Review*, February 1983, https://www.bls.gov/opub/mlr/1983/02/art1full.pdf.

[2] Daniel Kurt, "Historical Unemployment Rate by Year," *Investopedia*, updated June 30, 2024, https://www.investopedia.com/historical-us-unemployment-rate-by-year-7495494.

[3] "The Gallup Survey on Success," *SellingPower*, February 2, 2010, https://www.sellingpower.com/2010/02/02/8526/the-gallup-survey-on-success.

[4] ResumeLab, *Generation Z and Work: Survey Report*, 2023, https://resumelab.com/career-advice/generation-z-and-work.

[5] Morning Consult, *Gen Z and Quiet Quitting: Trends and Behaviors 2024*, Morning Consult Pro, April 2024, https://pro.morningconsult.com/analysis/gen-z-quiet-quitting-trends-behaviors-2024.

Chapter 9: Relationships, Love, and Family in a Fast-Paced World

How real love matures, why endurance matters more than excitement, and how character—not chemistry—builds relationships that last.

In an age where you can meet someone, date them, and break up—all without leaving your phone—relationships have become faster, louder, and more fragile. Convenience has replaced patience. Options feel endless, but commitment feels rare. Yet beneath all that noise, one truth remains unchanged: love still matters, and so does loyalty.

For generations, building a life together meant showing up, keeping promises, and learning how to grow through the hard parts instead of walking away from them. Gen X learned that before dating apps, before social media, and before "ghosting" became a verb. If you wanted a relationship, you had to pick up the phone, drive across town, and have the courage to face another person in real time.

But I'll be the first to admit—I'm probably not the best source for relationship advice. I wasn't the guy who married his high-school sweetheart and is looking forward to one day celebrating their fiftieth anniversary. In fact, I did the opposite. I avoided serious relationships all through high school. I didn't have my first real girlfriend until my junior year of college—and that didn't last long. My excuse was that I wanted to focus on my career. In Oklahoma, where many of my friends got married right out of high school, I wanted something different: college, the Air Force, maybe even becoming an astronaut or a general someday. Getting tied down didn't fit into that plan.

Of course, that story was also a convenient one. It gave me permission to date around, to keep everything casual, and to avoid the kind of responsibility that comes with truly investing in another person. By the time I'd been in the Air Force for four years, I finally met someone—and I ignored every red flag. I dove straight into marriage with the same mindset that had guided every other decision: when I wanted the light switch on, I flipped it on; when I didn't, I turned it off. At twenty-seven, I decided it was time to have that light on permanently, so I made a list of what I thought I wanted in a partner. But that list was shallow—a reflection of a twenty-something chasing a fantasy, not a man ready to build a life.

Looking back, I may have more in common with Gen Z than I thought. Today, among Gen Z adults, many remain open to marriage—but often on their own terms and at their own pace. For example, **69% of never-married young adults (ages 18–34)** say they want to get married someday, while **8% say they do not**, and **23% are unsure** when or if they will.[1] However, data aimed more at Gen Zers, appears even more dismal, with sources suggesting that only **58 % of Gen Z women and 56 % of Gen Z men** will ever marry at all (not just by a certain age).[2] That's a dramatic change in just a few years. At the same time, economic pressures and priority shifts appear to drive postponement: younger adults cite cost, career, and financial stability as key reasons to delay.[3] What does appear authentic within Gen Z is that only a minority embraces early marriage.

Gen Z men, in particular, are increasingly hesitant to commit—often citing financial insecurity, fear of divorce, or distrust of traditional gender roles. Many young men admit that they feel unprepared to be providers or partners in a world that continually shifts the standards for success. Add in online dating, unrealistic social-media standards, and the easy access to digital substitutes like pornography or platforms such as OnlyFans, and it's no wonder genuine intimacy feels harder to find.

But this chapter isn't about convincing anyone to repeat my mistakes—it's about recognizing those same human tendencies in ourselves. The propensity to chase excitement instead of substance. To avoid vulnerability under the guise of freedom. To confuse fun with fulfillment and physical attraction with emotional connection.

True love and lasting relationships demand more than chemistry—they require character. They ask you to take responsibility for someone else's well-being and, eventually, for the family you might build together. Those are things young men often avoid during adolescence but crave, even *need*, as they mature into adulthood.

Today's world moves faster than ever. Career goals come first, marriage comes later, and family often feels like something you "get to eventually." However, no matter how much the landscape changes, our need for belonging, partnership, and unconditional support remains constant. Technology can accelerate connection, but it can't replace meaning.

This chapter is about slowing down long enough to recognize what truly lasts. It's about rediscovering respect, commitment, and genuine care—the things that make love endure through busy schedules and digital distractions. A little bit of "old-school" chivalry and intentional effort can still set you apart in a world built on shortcuts.

Because when everything moves too fast, the real act of rebellion isn't chasing something new—it's staying long enough to build something real.

For those of us who grew up in Generation X, relationships looked a lot different. We didn't swipe right—we showed up.

If you liked someone, you had to actually talk to them. You called their house phone, rehearsed what you were going to say, and prayed their dad didn't answer. Dates were planned days in advance, not confirmed with a text ten minutes before. And if you got lost on the way to pick someone up, you pulled out a paper map or stopped at a gas station to ask for directions.

Breakups hurt too—but they were personal. You couldn't ghost someone or hide behind a screen. You had to look them in the eye, stumble through your explanation, and deal with the silence that followed. You didn't get to delete people; you had to face them. That kind of honesty forced us to grow thicker skin, but it also gave us deeper roots. Commitment wasn't about perfection—it was about sticking through imperfection.

I got my first hard lesson in relationships when I was thirteen. There was this girl—let's call her Jenny—whom I had the biggest crush on. I don't even remember her last name, but I'll never forget how it all played out. Looking back, I guess you'd say I was a "simp," long before the term existed—willing to do anything for a girl's attention, even if it was just to be noticed.

I spent most of my weeks at school trying to figure out where Jenny would be on the weekend so I could "accidentally" show up. Keep in mind, this was small-town Oklahoma—no cell phones, no texting, just word of mouth and teenage optimism. Sometimes that meant walking forty-five minutes, sometimes over an hour, just for the chance of seeing her.

For about three months, I kept this up—sometimes finding her, sometimes walking home alone in the dark. Then one night, I showed up at a local event where she happened to be. I hung nearby, hoping she'd notice me, and everything would magically fall into place. Instead, she finally turned around, clearly frustrated, and said, "Jeff, I don't like you. I don't want to date you. And I want you to stop following me everywhere."

That walk home felt a lot longer than an hour. I was humiliated, heartbroken, and angry. Something in me flipped that night. I told myself I'd never be the nice guy again. For the next couple of years, I went to the opposite extreme—what you might call the "pimp" approach. I played the game, treated girls like trophies, and convinced myself that being in control meant I couldn't be hurt again. And I'll admit—it worked, at least on the surface. The attention came easily. But it was hollow. I was counting achievements instead of building relationships.

Eventually, I met someone I genuinely liked, but by then my habits had already taken hold. I hurt her before the relationship even had a chance to start. That was my second wake-up call. I realized that neither extreme—simp nor pimp—led anywhere worth going. But back then, we didn't learn those lessons through screens or messages. We learned them face-to-face. I *felt* Jenny's disgust in person when she called me out. I *felt* the false sense of power in person, being the one in control. And I *felt in person* the shame of breaking someone's heart just because she had genuine feelings for me. Those emotions shaped me in ways that social media reactions never could.

That was the world we grew up in—where you had to experience rejection, remorse, and redemption in person. It made relationships raw, but real.

I didn't always value substance over excitement. In my twenties, I was chasing big dreams and bigger names. I wanted to be the next Bill Gates, Neil Armstrong, or maybe George Patton. Ambition was my fuel, and I measured my worth by the next challenge or promotion that lay ahead. But somewhere in my early thirties, the meaning of success began to shift.

I remember the day my oldest son took his first steps and the first time he said, "Dad." Those moments changed everything. They reframed what mattered most in life. A few years later, with three sons, I was promoted to lieutenant colonel in the Air Force, and I realized I had reached the peak of what I truly wanted. Sure, I could've chased full colonel, but it meant checking boxes—professional military education, certain assignments, and all the politics that came with it. I made a conscious choice to stop chasing those boxes. I chose instead to anchor myself where I was and put my family first.

That decision didn't come easy. I had spent two decades driven by excitement—by motion, ambition, and adrenaline. But the real turning point came when I realized that what I once called "drive" was often just a distraction. The things that lasted—my family, my kids, the people who loved me—were the ones that required my time, not my résumé.

That decision to shift, from chasing excitement to building substance, mirrored a change I now see many in Gen Z facing. You can pursue every dream, every passion, every side hustle—but none of it replaces the deep fulfillment that comes from commitment and purpose. The lesson isn't to stop dreaming; it's to make sure those dreams are tied to something that lasts.

Our generation also learned a lot from our parents' marriages—both their successes and their failures. Many of us grew up watching couples stay together through struggle, sometimes out of love, sometimes out of duty. We admired their resilience but also recognized their silence. They endured, but they didn't always communicate. We wanted to find balance—to keep the commitment but add emotional honesty.

That's where Gen X landed: halfway between our parents' sense of obligation and the next generation's search for authenticity. We learned that love isn't about finding the right person—it's about *becoming* the right person. Commitment doesn't come from luck; it comes from growth, humility, and staying when it would be easier to leave.

And maybe that's the lesson worth passing on. The relationships that last aren't built on convenience—they're built on courage, patience, and the willingness to grow together.

Every generation faces its own version of the same growing pains: wanting independence, craving connection, and chasing happiness before understanding what it truly is. Gen X and Gen Z are no different in that regard. The tools and culture have changed, but the inner struggles remain surprisingly similar.

Both generations value authenticity. We both question authority, push back against outdated traditions, and seek relationships that feel *real*. Neither wants to settle for superficiality. But where Gen X had fewer distractions, Gen Z has an entire digital universe competing for their attention. We learned about heartbreak face-to-face; they experience it through phones, DMs, and disappearing messages.

At twenty-three, I thought I was free. I packed my stuff into a car and drove thirteen hundred miles to rural Oklahoma—chasing a nostalgic dream of lake parties, beer, and aimless fun. I told myself I was escaping the grind, that I was living free—no schedule, no responsibilities, just endless summer.

It initially felt like freedom, but it wasn't. It was a lack of direction. Nothing is fulfilling about acting like a teenager in your twenties. I was trying to relive something that no longer existed, confusing movement with meaning. The truth is, I wasn't chasing happiness—I was running from fear. I was afraid of growing up, fearful of failure. I worried that taking on responsibility would mean the end of my fun.

What I was really doing was hiding from the future under the illusion of adventure. That same tendency is evident today in Gen Z, although the setting has changed. Instead of lakes and pickup trucks, it's Tinder and Instagram. Instead of boredom, it's constant stimulation. But the root is the same—confusing pleasure for purpose.

Biology even gives it a boost. Neuroscientists have found that during adolescence and early adulthood, the **prefrontal cortex**—the part of the brain that manages decision-making, impulse control, and long-term planning—is still developing well into the mid-20s. Meanwhile, the **limbic system**, which drives reward, emotion, and pleasure, is fully active and powerful.[4] That imbalance makes young adults—especially men—more prone to risk-taking, novelty-seeking, and instant gratification.

Simply put, the brain's gas pedal develops long before its brakes. The thrill of a new relationship, a party, or a spontaneous road trip feels good because the brain floods itself with dopamine. The same chemical reinforces pleasure and excitement. But without a fully developed sense of foresight, it's easy to mistake *pleasure* for *purpose*.

That's precisely what I did at twenty-three. I thought fun would bring happiness, but what I was really doing was avoiding my fear of the future. I wasn't ready to commit to anything—not a career, not a partner, not even a direction. I wanted happiness without responsibility. The freedom I was chasing was actually fear wearing an adventurous mask.

And that's where I see the parallel today. When I look at Gen Z, I recognize the same internal conflict—wanting connection but fearing commitment, craving meaning but settling for distraction. The difference is that the temptations now are supercharged. The dopamine hits come faster and easier—likes, swipes, instant messages, instant validation. Social media gives the illusion of being connected without ever requiring vulnerability. Dating apps offer endless choices but no accountability. You can always swipe to the next person before you ever have to face rejection or self-reflection.

But beneath it all, Gen Z isn't so different from where we were. They're searching for identity, for belonging, for something worth building a life around. They're growing up in a world that moves faster and demands more. Still, the core struggle remains timeless: how to turn youthful freedom into mature purpose.

The lesson I learned from that Oklahoma trip—and from the many mistakes that followed—is that freedom without direction eventually becomes emptiness. You can't find purpose in running away from responsibility or commitment. Real freedom isn't the absence of limits; it's the ability to choose what's worth pledging to.

That's the bridge between our generations: Gen X learned those lessons the hard way—face-to-face, one scar at a time. Gen Z has the opportunity to learn them sooner—if they can slow down long enough to recognize the difference between pleasure and fulfillment.

By the time I reached my late twenties, I thought I had life figured out. I had a solid career, a steady paycheck, and enough confidence to believe I was ready to get married. The truth is, I wasn't prepared for marriage—I was ready for what I *thought* marriage was supposed to be.

I want to be careful not to paint a bad picture of my ex-wife, the mother of my three wonderful sons. There were good reasons I married her. Molly was beautiful, full of life, and at twenty-seven, I was drawn to that energy. Coming off my own adolescent roller coaster, I could offer her adventure, travel, and a stable paycheck. We loved doing fun things together—weekend trips, new restaurants, spontaneous plans. But deep down, I knew the red flags were there from the beginning. She was high-maintenance, needed constant affirmation and gifts, and I convinced myself that was fine. That's on me.

I was set on marrying someone who checked all the boxes: good-looking, fun, and willing to follow my Air Force career. The problem was that my list was written by a boy, not a man. I was still thinking in terms of attraction and adventure, not longevity and partnership. At that stage of my life, I confused excitement with love, chemistry with compatibility, and charm with character.

When Molly and I got married, the chemistry was undeniable. We laughed, we traveled, and we shared a sense of excitement about the future. But as time passed and life began demanding more—late nights with sick kids, tight budgets, career moves, and the emotional work of parenting—the spark wasn't enough. That's when character had to take over. Someone had to stop spending on fun things and start saving for the future. Someone had to put away dreams of constant adventure and focus on building stability. Someone had to grow up.

And here's the truth: Molly didn't change—I did. The need for sex became the need for intimacy. The need for fun evolved into a need for partnership. The need to spend became the need to build. As I matured, I realized that true love and lasting relationships demand more than chemistry—they require *character.*

When life gets hard, someone must make sacrifices. Someone must give up weekends of fun to care for a sick child or save for a future. Someone must show up when it's inconvenient and stay when it's uncomfortable. That's where real love is tested.

When responsibility started to outweigh recreation, our marriage began to fracture. We had been built on chemistry and excitement, not endurance and shared growth. When the marriage finally broke up, I was forced to take a hard look at myself. What I saw wasn't failure—it was transformation.

It's not a story about blame; it's a story about *evolution.* Relationships don't fail because they lose chemistry—they fail when one person grows up and the other refuses to. I had to become someone new. The experience forced me to grow into a man who finally understood that love isn't about getting what you want—it's about giving what's needed.

And that's what I tell young men today: love is not found in the moments that feel easy; it's forged in the moments that test your patience, empathy, and resolve. True love requires maturity, sacrifice, and responsibility. It asks you to take responsibility for someone else's well-being—to protect something bigger than yourself.

Looking back now, I can see that growing into that kind of love was part of my journey to becoming a man. In my twenties, I needed affirmation. In my thirties, I needed exhilaration. But by my forties, I needed purpose. The relationships that endure—the ones that give life meaning—are built on respect, commitment, and genuine care.

I don't keep in touch with many of my "fun" friends from high school or college, but I've never lost touch with my family or my sons. Those relationships outlasted every promotion, every trip, every short-lived thrill. They're proof that the most valuable things in life can't be bought. They're built—one act of loyalty, one hard conversation, one promise kept at a time.

And if there's one piece of practical advice I'd offer, it's this: **a little bit of old-school chivalry and intentional effort still go a long way.** Even in my worst dating days—when I was immature and selfish—I still tried to make the other person feel special. Maya Angelou once said, *"People will forget what you said, people will forget what you did, but people will never forget how you made them feel."*

That quote captures something timeless. Today's culture sometimes treats respect and masculinity as outdated—but I see it differently. Chivalry isn't about control; it's about *character.* It's about men holding themselves to a higher standard of honor, courtesy, and responsibility. In a world where cynicism and mistrust come easily, being a gentleman takes real strength.

So, if you want to stand out, don't just chase attraction—be the man who brings safety, respect, and stability into the room. Be the example others look to. That's what it means to be "the man"—not the loudest or flashiest, but the one who makes others feel valued and secure.

That's how good relationships start—and how great ones endure.

When I look back on my life so far, the moments that stand out aren't the promotions, the paychecks, or the places I've been. They're the people I've shared it with—the family I built, the friends who stayed, and the sons who taught me more about love and patience than any adult ever could.

Love, family, and legacy are the quiet constants in a world that moves too fast. They don't trend. They don't go viral. But they endure. The greatest reward in life isn't found in what we accomplish—it's found in who we become through the relationships we choose to invest in.

The truth is, time has a way of revealing what really matters. The excitement fades, the noise dies down, and all that remains are the people who loved you enough to walk beside you through the most complex parts. In my twenties, I thought love was about passion. In my thirties, I thought it was about partnership. By my forties, I realized it was about presence—being there, every day, in the ordinary moments that make up a life.

That realization came into complete focus when I met my current wife, Kamma. If Molly, my first wife, represented my youthful chase for excitement and attraction, Kamma represented everything I didn't even realize I needed. She was, in many ways, Molly's opposite—and that was both good and challenging. What first drew me to Kamma wasn't romance in the Hollywood sense. It was something more profound, quieter, more mature. She was fiscally responsible, emotionally stable, and grounded. She was reliable as a co-parent and faithful as a partner.

At the time, I was on uncertain financial ground, facing the end of one career and the unknown of another. I had three elementary-aged boys depending on me, and I wasn't about to share that responsibility lightly. Looking back, I'm still amazed she found anything remotely attractive about me. Some might question the lack of a romantic tone in how we began, but that's because romance wasn't what we were building.

I remember telling Kamma early on that I wanted nothing to do with a woman who needed constant romance in her life. I said to her that romance dies the moment a man starts carrying out the household trash. What I needed wasn't flowers and candlelight—I needed someone who would still be there when life got difficult. Someone who wouldn't run when things got heavy.

And life *did* get difficult.

There was the time Julian, my oldest, was rushed into emergency surgery after dislocating his clavicle so severely it pressed against an artery, creating a blood clot that could've taken his life. That injury ended his football season, but could have ended much more. Kamma was there—steady, calm, supportive—helping me balance fear and fatherhood.

Then came Quinn's battle with mental health. I'll never forget the phone call telling me he'd tried to take his own life. I remember the helplessness of that drive to the hospital, the sleepless nights afterward, and the gut-wrenching decision to use half my retirement to send him to a treatment center three states away—because the insurance company wouldn't cover genuine adolescent care, only over-prescribed medication. Again, Kamma was there—shouldering the weight with me, never wavering.

And then there was Ian—our youngest—testing the limits of independence, determined to prove at nineteen that he could make it on his own. Navigating the chaos of a learning disability, anger, and frustration, he made our lives harder than either of us expected. But Kamma stayed. She loved him anyway, stood by me through every parent-teacher meeting, every slammed door, every late-night worry.

It's for these reasons, not despite them, that I asked Kamma to marry me. I didn't need someone to have fun with—I needed someone to *endure* with. Someone to grow old with, to share the good days and survive the bad ones. It may not sound sexy, but it's real. It's lasting. It's love that's been tested and proven.

And that's the lesson I want to leave with you: **the most meaningful relationships aren't built on excitement—**

they're built on endurance. You don't need a fairy tale; you need a foundation.

That's the irony of modern relationships: everyone's searching for something extraordinary, but the most incredible thing you can do is commit to someone ordinary—and love them consistently over time. It's not glamorous, but it's real.

For Gen Z, living in a fast-paced, hyperconnected world, the temptation will always be to chase what's next—to look for the next spark, the next thrill, the next validation. However, it is the people who find true fulfillment who are the ones who slow down long enough to build something lasting. The ones who choose depth over distraction.

Don't mistake motion for meaning. Don't confuse attraction for connection. And don't trade the quiet peace of genuine love for the fleeting rush of digital attention. The relationships that will define your life won't come from perfect timing or perfect compatibility—they'll come from perseverance, honesty, and care.

And that's where *legacy* comes in. Your greatest legacy won't be what you own—it'll be who you've loved. It won't be your résumé or your rank—it'll be the memories you leave behind in the hearts of others.

If you take anything from this chapter, let it be this: love isn't found in grand gestures; it's built through small, daily choices. Choose to show up. Choose to listen. Choose to forgive. Choose to build something that lasts.

Because when the noise fades and the world slows down, you'll find that the most meaningful things in life aren't the ones you can buy or post about—they're the ones you can hold.

So call the people you love. Tell them what they mean to you. Put down the phone long enough to look someone in the eye and say, *I'm here.* Because in a world that's forgotten what it means to commit, the most rebellious act of love is simply staying.

And always keep in mind that, **“In a world that swipes left too fast—choose to stay.”**

---

[1] Pew Research Center, “Among young adults without children …” (2024). Pew Research Center

[2] Benson, “The Collapse of Marriage Among Gen Z,” Marriage Foundation (2024).

[3] “Redefining ‘I Do’: Marital Attitudes Among Generation Z,” senior thesis, University of South Carolina (2024), which finds Gen Zers frequently defer marriage in favor of financial stability, career goals, and personal development. Scholar Commons

[4] *Steinberg, L. (2008). “A Social Neuroscience Perspective on Adolescent Risk-Taking.” Developmental Review,* 28(1), 78–106. https://doi.org/10.1016/j.dr.2007.08.002

Chapter 10: Personal Freedom and Responsibility

The Gen X mindset of 'no one is coming to save you,' understanding that with freedom comes responsibility, and how to own your choices in life.

Freedom has become one of the most overused and least understood words in our culture. Everyone wants it, but few talk about the cost that comes with it. Gen X learned early that freedom isn't about doing whatever you want—it's about owning whatever comes next.

We were the "latchkey generation." We came home to empty houses, made our own dinners, and figured things out without YouTube tutorials or a parent on standby. There was no rescue plan—if the bike chain broke, you walked it home. If you didn't study for the test, you failed. Somewhere in that independence, we absorbed a truth that still guides us today: **no one is coming to save you.**

That mindset wasn't cynical—it was empowering. It meant our success or failure wasn't waiting on luck, policy, or permission. It was in our hands. Freedom wasn't a gift; it was a responsibility. And responsibility wasn't punishment—it was power.

I saw that truth reinforced throughout my military career. In the service, we live in a constant cycle of planning and training for what might happen. We don't do it because we expect disaster every day—we do it because our job is to be ready when war and conflict comes. War is uncertain, but preparation isn't. "Prepping," as civilians like to call it, is second nature to anyone in uniform. You learn quickly that when things go wrong, you don't get to point fingers or wait for someone else to fix it. You act, you adapt, and you overcome. Freedom and readiness are two sides of the same coin.

That lesson came into sharper focus for me after Hurricane Katrina in 2005. Like most Americans, I watched in disbelief as parts of New Orleans descended into chaos—violence, looting, and heartbreak—while nearby towns in Mississippi, Alabama, and the Florida panhandle, which had suffered even greater physical destruction, somehow held together. I kept asking myself why. What made the difference?

The answer, though uncomfortable, was clear. In New Orleans, many people had become overly reliant on the government for their day-to-day survival. When that system failed, panic filled the void. In smaller towns, people leaned on each other, took initiative, and relied on the same instincts that come from personal responsibility. They didn't wait to be saved—they started saving themselves.

That realization stuck with me so profoundly that my first attempt at writing a book was a fictional story about a future America fractured by its own dependence—a nation that, after exhausting the resources of the federal government, collapsed under the weight of its expectations. The question that inspired it came straight from the aftermath of Katrina: *What happens when we trade responsibility for comfort, and the safety net finally breaks?*

This chapter is about that balance—the freedom to do what you want and the responsibility to live with what you've done. It's a reminder that true liberty isn't measured by how much you can get away with but by how well you can stand on your own when everything else falls apart.

Because when you finally stop waiting for someone to save you, you start saving yourself—and that's when freedom really begins.

For Gen X, freedom wasn't a political slogan or a philosophical concept—it was a daily necessity. We didn't grow up in a world that coddled us or cushioned us from discomfort. We were raised to adapt, to improvise, and to figure things out on our own. The world didn't hand us participation trophies—it gave us problems to solve.

To better understand that mindset, it helps to look at the wider American climate we matured in. In the late 1970s, the country was struggling—stagflation, energy crises, crisis of confidence. The Iran hostage crisis during Jimmy Carter's presidency became a national symbol of weakness: 52 American diplomats and citizens held for 444 days, a failed rescue mission that cost lives, and a palpable sense that the U.S. was no longer invincible. The inability, or perceived inability, of the government to project strength or protect its own shook the national psyche.

Then came Ronald Reagan. His arrival wasn't just about policy—it was about restoring belief. With campaign slogans like "Let's make America great again" and the iconic "Morning in America" ads, Reagan tapped into a longing for renewal and optimism. The rhetoric framed America as a beacon again, a country to be admired and trusted. Whether or not every promise matched reality, the shift in mood was real. A more confident America to many meant more freedom in spirit—and more faith in one's own stake in that freedom.

Even public sentiment reflected this shift. During Reagan's presidency, his favorable ratings stayed strong (in the 60-percent range) among many Americans.[1] Polls from the 1980s suggest a resurgence in national pride and the framing of nationalism in more overt, positive terms.[2] That cultural shift—a renewed faith in the American promise—helped create fertile ground for a generation raised on self-reliance rather than collective rescue.

We came of age in the 1970s and '80s, when both parents worked, the divorce rate spiked, and the term "latchkey kid" entered the national vocabulary. After school, we'd unlock the front door, make our own snack, and manage a few hours of independence before Mom or Dad got home. We learned early that life didn't pause just because we were young. There was a quiet expectation that we'd be fine—and somehow, we were.

That experience became our foundation. It taught us that freedom doesn't come from being protected—it comes from being trusted. When no one is there to fix your problems, you learn how to fix them yourself. We rode bikes without helmets, explored woods without GPS, and stayed out until the streetlights came on. We didn't always make wise decisions, but every mistake became a lesson. And those lessons, collected over years of small risks and small recoveries, built a kind of resilience no textbook could teach.

By the time we entered adulthood, the economy was volatile, technology was changing, and the old guarantees—steady jobs, lifetime pensions, affordable housing—were vanishing. Gen X had to learn to navigate uncertainty. Many of us transitioned from analog childhoods to digital adulthood: rotary phones to smartphones, handwritten résumés to online job platforms, stable careers to shifting gig and contract economies. No one taught us how to make that leap—we just did. Adaptability wasn't optional; it was survival.

That independence carried over into how we viewed responsibility. We grew up hearing phrases like "you made your bed, now lie in it" and "life's not fair—deal with it." Harsh, maybe—but effective. It taught us that consequences weren't personal attacks; they were part of the deal. Freedom and responsibility were never separate ideas—they were one and the same. You could make your own choices, but you also had to own the fallout.

I've lived that lesson more than once. When I found myself back in Oklahoma with only a few dollars in my pocket, I didn't expect the government—or my parents—to come bail me out. When I got laid off years later, yes, unemployment benefits helped bridge the gap, but I never saw it as a permanent support system. Within days, I was already working on a plan to rebuild. I didn't want sympathy; I wanted momentum. That mindset—of adapting, rebuilding, and moving forward—became my default setting.

It's why I struggled to understand how so many people could become as helpless as those in New Orleans after Hurricane Katrina. I started digging into that question, not out of judgment, but curiosity. What makes one community resilient while another collapses under pressure? That question became a mental exercise, and eventually the foundation for a personal project—my own *concept of operations* or **CONOPS**, as we'd call it in the military. I began studying historical examples of nations that fell apart, what replaced them, and how freedom and responsibility played pivotal roles in each of these stories. Those notes evolved into character development and, eventually, the early chapters of what would become a book.

One of the most striking inspirations came from a story told by Shannon, the millennial I hired who was taking night classes at a local community college. In one of her classes, the professor led a discussion about what might happen if the government temporarily shut down and welfare checks were delayed. It was just a hypothetical scenario meant to spark critical thinking—nothing political, nothing personal. But one woman in the class—who was living entirely on government assistance—completely melted down. The very idea that her government benefits might stop, even for a week, was unthinkable to her. She shouted that such a thing could never happen, and that the professor shouldn't even bring it up.

That story stuck with me. For most of us, complete dependence on the government seems unimaginable; yet, for others, it has become a way of life so deeply ingrained that even questioning it feels threatening. The fear of losing that safety net—real or imagined—has grown into a kind of modern captivity. And that dependence, I realized, isn't limited to social programs. Many of us, in one form or another, become dependent on employers, institutions, technology, and even relationships. Freedom is eroded one small compromise at a time, until we forget what independence truly feels like.

That became the central theme of my fictional book, and the thread that connected every character I wrote. They weren't fighting external enemies so much as internal ones—fear, complacency, and dependence. It turns out that freedom and responsibility aren't just personal virtues—they're the bedrock of every functioning society. When either breaks down, collapse isn't far behind.

And that's the lesson Gen X learned firsthand: personal freedom isn't about isolation—it's about competence. The more capable you become, the more control you have over your own life. Freedom without capability is just wishful thinking. Our generation's approach was simple—if you want independence, earn it. Build the skills, make the effort, and be prepared to shoulder the responsibilities that come with standing on your own two feet.

That's the lesson worth passing on—not because we had it harder, but because we learned how to rely on ourselves and still make it through. Freedom isn't something someone gives you; it's something you grow into. And once you do, it's the most empowering feeling in the world.

Every generation claims to value freedom, but few stop to ask what kind of freedom they actually want—or what they're willing to trade for it. For Gen X, freedom was about survival and obtaining security. For Gen Z, it's about identity—and, increasingly, affordability: a home, healthcare, and a future that feels within reach. The two are not enemies, but they stem from very different worlds and assumptions about what it means to be independent.

Gen X grew up in an analog world that required effort and self-correction. If something broke, you fixed it. If you wanted to talk to someone, you picked up a phone—or knocked on their door. Nothing was instantaneous, and that delay taught patience, problem-solving, and consequence. We didn't have the luxury of outsourcing our daily lives to devices, corporations, or governments. Freedom was inseparable from responsibility because no one else was going to show up for you.

Gen Z, on the other hand, has been raised in an age of abundance and immediacy. Nearly everything is one click, one tap, or one algorithm away. The modern world has promised this generation convenience, access, and customization on a scale that we couldn't have imagined. But hidden within that promise is a trap—the gradual surrender of personal control in exchange for comfort. The more systems we rely on to think, plan, or decide for us, the easier it becomes to confuse dependency for progress.

That trade-off—relinquishing freedom for the promise of safety, ease, or fairness—isn't new. It's a recurring theme throughout history. Human nature tends to gravitate toward security, even when that security comes at the cost of autonomy. Gen X saw it in the form of government expansion, corporate paternalism, and cultural messaging that said the "system" would take care of you if you followed the rules. Gen Z faces it through digital infrastructure, social-media influence, and institutional guarantees that claim to remove all risk from life.

However, long before Gen X—or even the Baby Boomers—this same mindset justified one of the darkest chapters in American history. In the antebellum South, pro-slavery advocates claimed that enslavement was a *benevolent institution*. Thinkers like **George Fitzhugh**, author of *A Pro-Slavery Argument (1857),* insisted that enslaved people were "better off" under the care of their masters, receiving food, housing, and "moral instruction" in exchange for their labor. [3] Others, such as Episcopal Bishop **John Henry Hopkins** in his 1861 pamphlet *A Scriptural, Ecclesiastical, and Historical View of Slavery,* went further—arguing that slavery was not only legal under Scripture but "beneficial" to those held in bondage.[4]

These arguments reframed oppression as kindness—dependency masquerading as protection. The same human instinct that fears uncertainty will often accept subjugation if it's branded as security. The language of care, provision, and stability becomes the moral cloak for control. That pattern didn't end with emancipation; it simply evolved.

A century later, America's political and cultural identity underwent another transformation. Many today know the story as the "Southern Strategy"—the idea that the Republican Party reinvented itself to attract disaffected white voters through coded racial appeals. But as political historian **Kevin Phillips** and others have shown, the deeper reality was more complex. Books like *The Big Switch* argue that the South's political shift from Democratic to Republican dominance was driven far more by *economic policy, cultural values, and the resurgence of individualism under Reagan* than by race alone.

The South didn't "switch" because one party suddenly became racist—it shifted because many voters sought a message of *self-determination over dependency,* a return to the belief that prosperity flowed from work and responsibility, not government patronage. The political labels changed, but the underlying human tension remained the same: freedom versus control, self-reliance versus promised security.

That same pattern echoes today, though the stage looks different. Where plantation owners once claimed to provide "care," governments now claim to provide "rights." Where mid-century political machines promised stability through social programs, today's tech giants promise safety through algorithms. The rationalization hasn't changed—just the packaging. Each generation must decide whether it will remain free or trade liberty for the illusion of comfort.

And hovering over all of this is a broader global lesson—one repeated again and again through the 20th century. The ideologies of **socialism** and **communism** often arrive not with violence, but with promises that sound compassionate and fair. Their introductions are almost always peaceful and appealing: free healthcare, guaranteed housing, universal income, and state-managed equality. For those struggling to gain a foothold in modern life, such offers sound humane, even moral. But history reminds us that these bargains carry a hidden cost—one paid in freedom.

Communism's record speaks for itself: wherever it has fully taken root, it has demanded control of property, speech, religion, and ultimately the individual. Socialism, while often softer in tone, follows a similar trajectory—starting with benevolence and ending with dependence. Its early messaging—*"We'll take care of you; you won't have to struggle"*—is enticing precisely because it appeals to our instinct for safety. But once personal responsibility is traded for state provision, the individual's power to choose, question, and dissent gradually erodes. The lesson for any free society is clear: the more authority you give away in exchange for comfort, the less of yourself you'll have left to protect when that comfort disappears.

It's a pattern as old as civilization—freedom offered up for security, autonomy surrendered for promises of care. And it always begins with noble words: *equality, fairness, compassion.* Yet history warns us that freedom rarely dies in battle; it fades through complacency.

Freedom is never free, and it's never permanent. It requires vigilance, courage, and self-discipline to maintain. Gen X learned that lesson through trial and error; Gen Z is learning it in real time through the subtle erosion of privacy, autonomy, and choice. The question isn't whether the world will change—because it always does—but whether each generation will have the courage to remain free when change tempts them to surrender.

That's where our stories intersect: both generations are standing on opposite ends of the same bridge. One side built freedom through hardship; the other is being asked to defend it through awareness. And the more we understand that link, the better chance we have of breaking humanity's oldest habit —the urge to trade freedom for comfort and call it progress.

Freedom isn't something a nation guarantees—it's something a person maintains. It doesn't erode overnight; it fades one compromise at a time. Every generation faces the same test: whether to stand guard over its liberty or to trade it away for comfort, convenience, or conformity.

As Ronald Reagan warned in his 1964 speech *A Time for Choosing*:

"Freedom is never more than one generation away from extinction. We didn't pass it to our children in the bloodstream. It must be fought for, protected, and handed on for them to do the same."

What Reagan meant was that liberty isn't genetic—it's cultural and moral. It survives only when each generation consciously chooses to defend it. For Gen Z, that message is urgent. You were born into unprecedented access, connectivity, and comfort—but that same environment dulls the instincts of vigilance. The fight for freedom today isn't on a battlefield; it's in the daily decisions to think independently, act responsibly, and refuse to be managed by systems that trade your autonomy for convenience.

Gen X learned this the hard way—living through the transition from analog to digital, from Cold War certainty to global interdependence, from self-reliance to systemic dependence. Gen Z will face the same test in a more connected but less grounded world.

The first defense of freedom isn't political—it's personal.

A free nation is only as strong as the number of free individuals it contains. And individuals remain free when they take responsibility in three key areas: **financial, intellectual, and civic life.**

1. Financial Responsibility: Freedom Requires Margin

You can't be free if you're financially trapped. Debt, consumerism, and short-term gratification are modern chains —just polished to look like prosperity. Every generation learns this lesson the hard way. Still, Gen Z has inherited a world where debt is normalized—from student loans to credit cards to "buy-now-pay-later" apps.

I had to learn this the hard way myself, and not early enough. Only now, in my late fifties—after layoffs, divorce, and even bankruptcy—am I finally reaching financial freedom. Each of those setbacks carried the same lesson: when you lose financial independence, you lose leverage over your own life.

Freedom starts with discipline. Live below your means. Invest in skills before stuff. Measure success not by income, but by independence. Money doesn't buy happiness, but it does buy options—and options are what keep you free. A person who manages their finances wisely can walk away from a bad boss, a corrupt system, or a failing relationship. Someone who can't is forced to endure them.

Financial readiness also allows you to seize opportunities when they appear. Downturns, recessions, or buyers' markets aren't times of despair—they're openings for those who prepared. Freedom favors those who plan ahead.

True financial freedom doesn't mean luxury; it means mobility—the ability to redirect your time and labor according to your values. Governments can promise equality, but they can't grant independence. That's something only earned through effort and restraint.

2. Intellectual Responsibility: Freedom Requires Thought

Every dictatorship begins by narrowing the range of acceptable ideas. When people stop thinking for themselves, someone else will gladly do it for them. In today's world, the threat isn't censorship by force—it's **distraction by design**.

Social-media algorithms don't need to silence you if they can keep you scrolling, entertained, and too exhausted to think deeply.

My own dark secret is that I spend too much time on iFunny reading the endless back-and-forth between generations and political parties. The same tired argument replays itself daily. The Left argues that the rich get richer while the poor get poorer. The Right counters that communism has failed everywhere it's been tried. The Left pivots to praise "social democracies" like Finland; the Right replies that Finland's socialist experiment faltered economically, forcing a return to more market-based policies. Then the debate collapses into insults—each side calling the other ignorant or evil—and everyone retreats to their digital corners.

It's a microcosm of modern intellectual laziness: endless noise, little depth. True debate requires curiosity, humility, and the patience to understand the opposing argument well enough to challenge it intelligently.

And it's true—both sides have valid points. The Left is correct that many of the ultra-rich continue to accumulate wealth while the poorest struggle. In truth it happens under liberal and conservative administrations and policies. The Right is correct that redistributive systems and planned economies historically fail to lift nations sustainably. The truth lies in nuance. Market capitalism produces innovation, but it also fosters inequality. Social safety nets can protect the vulnerable, but they can also easily breed dependency if left unchecked. A mature society must hold both truths and keep debating—not to win, but to improve.

This is why **understanding history, economics, and culture** matters. As **Winston Churchill** famously said before the British Parliament in 1947:

"No one pretends that democracy is perfect or all-wise. Indeed, it has been said that democracy is the worst form of government—except for all those other forms that have been tried from time to time."

Churchill's point applies not just to government but to discourse itself. Systems—and people—are flawed, but they remain the best tools we have if we keep refining them through honest debate.

Education doesn't end with a diploma; it begins there. Read original sources. Question easy narratives. Remember that freedom of speech means nothing if you're too uninformed—or too afraid—to use it.

3. Civic Responsibility: Freedom Requires Engagement

Freedom also depends on participation. In a republic, power doesn't disappear when you ignore it—it simply shifts to those who show up. Civic freedom isn't preserved through hashtags; it's preserved through engagement: voting, volunteering, attending local meetings, and paying attention to who writes the rules you live under.

You don't have to run for office to make an impact. Simply being an informed, active citizen is a revolutionary act in an age of apathy. Understand how your government works. Study the Constitution and the Bill of Rights—not as relics, but as living guardrails for liberty.

I learned this firsthand a few years ago when I got involved in my local caucus. What started as mild curiosity quickly evolved into an education on how democracy actually functions. I ended up becoming a delegate for my party and began attending local meetings—something I'd never imagined myself doing. It forced me to think differently, to choose not between parties but between people within my own. I had to evaluate which candidate best represented my values, not simply vote against someone else's. And that's when it hit me: local politics isn't some distant machine—it's a handful of ordinary citizens making real decisions that ripple outward. In some meetings, there were only a few hundred of us—sometimes fewer—deciding who would ultimately appear on the larger ballot. The experience taught me that civic influence doesn't come from shouting at the television or posting online; it comes from showing up.

As I discussed earlier in this book, **critical thinking** isn't about how much you know; it's about how well you know it. Some of the most effective debaters are those labeled as intolerant or outdated—not because they are right about everything, but because they've studied their opponents' ideas more deeply than their opponents have studied their own.

I often think of the late **Charlie Kirk**, who represented the belief that freedom demands engagement. His debates—thousands of them, peaceful, structured, and public—were models of intellectual endurance. When his critics could no longer counter his reasoning, they resorted to name-calling. Yet Charlie persisted, proving that the answer to bad arguments isn't censorship or violence, but better arguments and courage. His assassination was a tragic reminder that free speech always carries risk. The least we can do to honor that sacrifice is to keep talking—to debate without hatred, to listen without surrender, and to test our beliefs continually against new evidence.

Civic responsibility also means protecting the freedoms of others, even those with whom you disagree. Free speech, religion, and association only matter if they apply universally. Once we start deciding who *deserves* rights, freedom stops being a principle. It becomes a privilege—and privileges can be revoked.

The Modern Test of Freedom

Today, threats to freedom rarely arrive in uniform. They come disguised as convenience: free money, free healthcare, free housing—free everything but the freedom to choose otherwise. The messaging sounds compassionate, but history is unkind to societies that trade autonomy for guaranteed comfort. Once you exchange personal responsibility for state provision, it's nearly impossible to get it back.

The antidote isn't cynicism—it's competence. Build a life that doesn't depend on rescue. Learn to repair, create, invest, and adapt. Be the person your grandparents could count on, and your children will thank you for it.

Freedom isn't preserved by waiting for the right politician, party, or policy—it's preserved by the daily habits of ordinary people who refuse to surrender their will.

If nothing else, remember these key lessons:

Financial – Control your money, or it will control you.

Build margin in your life. Avoid debt when possible. Save when others spend. Invest when others panic. Financial discipline is what enables you to act with courage when opportunity or crisis arises. The person with cash reserves and low debt is the one who gets to choose—not the one who must beg.

Intellectual – Question everything, especially what flatters your biases.

Seek truth, not validation. Read history from multiple angles. Surround yourself with people who think differently, because sharpening ideas requires friction. Real freedom begins in the mind; protect it from laziness and propaganda alike.

Civic – Show up, speak up, and stand up—for yourself and for others.

Apathy is the silent killer of liberty. Be a participant, not a spectator. Defend the rights of even those you dislike, because if their freedoms fall today, yours may follow tomorrow.

Freedom has always required vigilance. Gen X earned it through endurance; Gen Z must protect it through awareness. The tools may differ, but the battle remains the same. The moment we forget that freedom demands effort, someone else will decide how much we're allowed to keep.

"No one is coming to save you—and that's your greatest advantage."

Freedom isn't a birthright; it's a responsibility. It isn't permanent, and it doesn't renew itself with each generation.

It must be fought for, protected, and passed down like a sacred inheritance. Ronald Reagan warned us in 1964 that *"freedom is never more than one generation away from extinction."* What he meant wasn't simply about politics—it was about people. Freedom survives only when individuals care enough to maintain it, to preserve it not as a trophy, but as a trust.

For Gen X, that lesson was learned through trial and error, often in the face of scarcity. We grew up with scraped knees and limited resources, and a clear understanding that no one was coming to bail us out. We learned the value of self-reliance the hard way—through layoffs, recessions, divorces, and sometimes bankruptcy. I've lived those seasons myself. There were times when I had to start over with nothing but determination and the understanding that responsibility was my only path back to freedom.

Gen Z faces a different challenge. You've inherited a world of abundance, connectivity, and convenience—but also one where independence can be quietly traded away in exchange for comfort. You don't have to fight a tyrant to lose your freedom; you only have to stop paying attention. Every tap, click, and shortcut that removes friction from your life also removes a small piece of your agency. The question is no longer whether you can be free—but whether you'll have the courage to stay free when the world makes it easy not to be.

True freedom isn't the absence of struggle—it's the ability to choose your path through it. It's financial discipline that lets you walk away from bad systems, intellectual rigor that keeps you from being manipulated, and civic engagement that ensures your voice still matters. Freedom dies in comfort long before it dies in conflict.

When I got involved in my local caucus, I realized how fragile democracy really is. I wasn't voting against anyone—I was helping decide who even appeared on the ballot. There were nights when fewer than a hundred of us were making decisions that would shape our city, our county, even our state. That experience opened my eyes to how few people truly engage, and how much power lies in the hands of those who show up. Civic responsibility doesn't require fame, wealth, or a title—it requires presence.

And presence is everything. Because when you stop showing up—financially, intellectually, civically—someone else steps in to make your choices for you. That's how freedom fades, not through conquest, but through neglect.

Churchill was right when he said, *"Democracy is the worst form of government—except for all those other forms that have been tried."* The same can be said of personal liberty. It's messy, difficult, and imperfect—but it's the only system that gives you the right to improve it. And improvement starts with you.

If my life has taught me anything, it's that freedom doesn't favor the strongest or the wealthiest—it favors the most responsible. The people who plan ahead. The ones who think critically. The ones who show up. Whether you're rebuilding after failure or just beginning your adult life, the formula hasn't changed: discipline + integrity + action = freedom.

So if you take one message from this chapter, let it be this:

Stop waiting for permission to live freely. You already have it.

Stop expecting others to fix what only you can repair.

Stop trading freedom for comfort and calling it progress.

Because freedom isn't a system—it's a habit. It's a daily choice. It's earned every time you think before you react, save before you spend, and speak when silence feels safer.

Reagan warned us that freedom can vanish in a single generation. Let's make sure that generation isn't yours. Teach your children what struggle feels like, so they understand what freedom costs. Challenge ideas instead of people. Learn history before you try to rewrite it. And above all—show up.

Because freedom isn't something you inherit. It's something you prove worthy of keeping.

---

[1] Gallup News. "*Ronald Reagan From the People's Perspective: Gallup Poll Review.*" Gallup, 2004. https://news.gallup.com/poll/11887/ronald-reagan-from-peoples-perspective-gallup-poll-review.aspx

[2] Roper Center for Public Opinion Research. "*American Pride: Public Opinion, 1974–1984.*" Cornell University, archived public data (Roper Report 1984-103021). https://ropercenter.cornell.edu/sites/default/files/2018-07/103021.pdf

[3] Fitzhugh, George. *A Pro-Slavery Argument: With Reference to the Actual Condition of the Slave in the Southern States*. Richmond, 1857.

[4] Hopkins, John Henry. *A Scriptural, Ecclesiastical, and Historical View of Slavery.* New York: W.I. Pooley & Co., 1861.

Chapter 11: The Inevitable Shift: Thriving During Failure

A look at how individuals, systems, or even nations rise — learning to embrace change and destructive technologies with innovation and accountability rather than fear and complacency.

One of the most notable differences I observe between Gen X and Gen Z revolves around books and reading. Growing up, my generation stood right at the cusp of the digital revolution. We still carried physical books, savored turning pages, and built mental stamina for long-form thinking. I can't tell you how many books I own that contain hundreds of lines highlighted in yellow or personal notes in the margins—a quiet dialogue between author and reader that lives forever in ink.

That kind of relationship with knowledge is fading, much like rotary-dial landlines and manual transmissions. We were the last generation to live before attention became a commodity. We watched the shift happen in real time—from deep reading and reflection to bite-sized content, memes, threads, and endless scrolling.

That shift is real and accelerating. A recent study reveals that daily reading for pleasure in the U.S. has declined by more than **40 percent over the past 20 years**—falling from approximately 28 percent of adults reading for leisure daily in 2003 to just 16 percent in 2023.[1] Moreover, in 2022, only about **48.5 percent of adults** reported having read at least one book in the past year, down from 52.7 percent just five years earlier.[2]

The cultural undercurrents driving this are numerous: shorter attention spans, constant notifications, algorithmically delivered content optimized for quick engagement, and a relentless competition for fleeting moments of time. We haven't lost access to ideas—we've simply changed the format. We now expect ideas to come in micro-snacks instead of full meals. In a world where clicks reward immediacy, deep reflection and sustained reading have become almost an act of rebellion.

I don't want this chapter—or this book—to become a lament about falling attention spans. Instead, I want to fight back. Over the following two chapters, I'm going to anchor our exploration in a few of my favorite works—books that helped shape how I think about freedom, responsibility, and the rise and fall of nations.

The first three are *Why Nations Fail* by Daron Acemoglu and James A. Robinson, *Democracy in America* by Alexis de Tocqueville, and *Good to Great* by Jim Collins. Much of what follows in this chapter draws inspiration from these works—their logic, stories, and conviction—but this isn't about just quoting or repeating them. My goal is to interpret their insights through a **Gen X lens**, translating timeless lessons about leadership, freedom, and discipline into a language that connects with a generation raised on memes and short clips.

If you sense the influence of those books in these pages, you're right—but I hope you also see something new: a perspective shaped by decades of systemic change, personal failure, and hard-won resilience. The intent isn't to worship great ideas but to **work** with them—to apply them, test them, and see what still holds true in a world that moves faster than ever.

So, let's not proceed as passive consumers of thought, but as **active builders of understanding**—readers who don't just absorb wisdom, but apply it.

Let me begin with my interpretation.

There's a city called Nogales that straddles the U.S.–Mexico border. The northern half, Nogales, Arizona, looks and feels like any other small American town—paved streets, public schools, stable utilities, and a police department that mostly keeps order. The southern half, Nogales, Sonora, sits just across a chain-link fence. The people there share the same climate, the same desert soil, even the same name—but life is harder. Wages are lower, corruption is higher, and opportunity is scarce.

It's a striking picture: one community divided not by geography or talent but by the systems they live under. *Why Nations Fail* uses Nogales to ask a larger question: why do some societies rise while others fall? The answer isn't luck or natural resources; it's the strength of their institutions and their willingness to adapt. Where rules are fair and people can innovate freely, progress thrives. Where power concentrates and fear of change sets in, decline follows.

It's an intriguing historical twist: Mexico, not long after independence, experimented with constitutions that mirrored republican systems—including elements borrowed from the U.S. and European liberal thought. In fact, early Mexican constitutions, such as the **Constitution of 1824**, adopted the structure of a federal republic and a representative government.[3] Political thinkers in 19th-century Mexico were well aware of U.S. models, and figures like **Stephen F. Austin** even circulated model drafts for Mexico's constitutional thinkers to consider.[4]

Yet despite adopting similar formal structures, Mexico did not end up on the same developmental trajectory as its northern neighbor. This divergence is a real-world illustration of a key lesson: institutions and design matter—but so does the character of the people who sustain them.

That insight was already visible to **Alexis de Tocqueville** when he traveled through the young United States and penned *Democracy in America* (first volumes published between 1835 and 1840). Tocqueville observed that laws and institutions alone could not explain why democracy succeeded in America; rather, it depended on the habits, civic virtues, social norms, and active engagement of citizens. In his view, the "soft infrastructure" of society—the willingness to participate, the culture of associating with others, the habits of self-governance—was as critical as any written constitution.

This question of democracy's endurance may seem like an odd issue to contemplate for someone born more than 200 years after the founding of America. But in the 18th and early 19th centuries, the success of a democracy surviving beyond its first generation was almost unheard of. Democracies tended to collapse soon after their creation—hence the old saying that "democracy is two wolves and a sheep deciding what's for dinner." Once the majority discovered it could vote itself the property of the minority, self-government usually imploded under the weight of human nature. Tocqueville recognized how unusual the American experiment truly was: a democracy that lasted because its people practiced restraint, cooperation, and civic duty.

That notion dovetails directly with *Why Nations Fail*. The same formal structure can exist on paper—but if citizens, elites, and institutions resist change or centralize control, the system will decay. History repeatedly shows that thriving societies are those where contributors remain creative, accountable, and open to renewal—not those that rest on formal rules alone.

Meanwhile, the patterns Tocqueville observed on the macro level are repeated in microcosm: in companies, communities, families, and individuals. Two people can live under the same laws, but one innovates, adapts, and invests in renewal while the other clings to the past and fades. That's the real lesson: systems—large or small—succeed when they stay open to renewal.

As a Gen Xer, I've lived through enough of these shifts to recognize the pattern. The Cold War ended, and whole industries were reshaped overnight. The dot-com boom exploded, then imploded. The housing crash tore through jobs and savings. Each time, the people who survived weren't the ones with the safest plans; they were the ones willing to rebuild faster than events could knock them down.

Our generation learned, sometimes the hard way, that failure isn't final—it's the moment evolution begins. And that same truth now faces Gen Z. Whether it's automation, artificial intelligence, or political gridlock, the institutions around us are creaking under the weight of change. The question isn't whether they'll fail—it's who will be ready to thrive when they do.

Because every collapse—national, economic, or personal—is also an invitation. The challenge is whether we see it as an ending or as the inevitable shift that clears the way for something better.

If there's one word that defines Gen X, it's *adaptation.* We grew up between two worlds—the analog and the digital, the old structure and the new frontier. We were raised by parents who prized stability but came of age in a world that guaranteed none. By the time we reached adulthood, the Cold War had ended, the global economy had shifted, and job security had been replaced by something far more demanding: personal agility.

In the military, corporate offices, or small businesses, the lesson was the same—change doesn't wait for your permission. You either evolved or you became obsolete. It's a truth I saw play out again and again: from the collapse of Soviet-style command economies to the rise of Silicon Valley, from dial-up internet to smartphones, from brick-and-mortar to remote everything. The world never slowed down again after Gen X entered it.

That's why *Why Nations Fail* struck such a deep chord with me. Its premise—that systems collapse when they stop adapting—wasn't just a theory about governments; it was a mirror held up to every generation that's faced change and hesitated. The authors describe how extractive institutions cling to control, suppress innovation, and inevitably rot from within. The inclusive ones, by contrast, invite participation, reward creativity, and adapt more quickly than crises can consume them.

That same tug-of-war between fear and progress has echoed through history. In *Why Nations Fail*, Acemoglu and Robinson describe how the Roman Empire's elite resisted the spread of labor-saving technologies, such as water-driven mills, fearing they would threaten the slave-based economy that preserved their wealth and power. Rather than embrace tools that could have multiplied productivity, they suppressed them to protect privilege—an act of self-preservation that, over time, helped doom the Empire's competitiveness.

Even centuries later, rulers continued to repeat the same mistake. In Elizabethan England, Queen Elizabeth I famously denied inventor William Lee a patent for his mechanical knitting frame in 1589, fearing that the machine would "tend to the ruin of many poor people."[5] Her decision temporarily safeguarded employment but ultimately delayed the innovation that later fueled the Industrial Revolution. The same tension replayed in every age: the automobile displacing livery-stable workers, tractors reducing the need for farmhands, computers eliminating clerical jobs. What seems like "destructive technology" in the moment almost always becomes the engine of greater prosperity once societies adapt.

That's what makes listening to Gen Z both fascinating and familiar. As they grapple with the promises and perils of artificial intelligence—sometimes fearing it will erode their livelihoods, sometimes embracing it as a form of liberation—

I can't help but hear the echoes of those older struggles. Every generation has confronted a technology that threatened to upend the way things were. For my generation it was the personal computer that threatened to take away the jobs of many white-collar workers but in reality, it would end up creating millions of new jobs in the IT sector and the need for software developers. The pattern never changes: fear dominates first, followed by adaptation, and then reinvention. The future belongs not to the ones who panic, but to those who learn how to partner with progress rather than resist it.

This is the same dynamic that played out in our own lives. The people and companies that thrived weren't always the smartest—they were the most disciplined, the most willing to face uncomfortable truths and change direction before circumstances forced them to. That, in a nutshell, is what Stanford professor Jim Collins called *disciplined adaptability* in his best-selling book *Good to Great*: the ability to evolve without losing focus or integrity.

Collins' research showed that great organizations don't survive upheaval by luck. They do it through what he called the "Flywheel"—a steady, deliberate momentum built on small, consistent actions that compound over time. They don't panic during change; they prepare for it. And when the world shifts—as it always does—they already have the habits, structures, and mindset to pivot without losing purpose.

That mirrors Tocqueville's observations in *Democracy in America*. When he toured the United States in the 1830s, he observed a young nation constantly reinventing itself—yet somehow managing to hold together. What fascinated him wasn't the written Constitution; it was the invisible framework of personal responsibility and civic virtue. Americans formed associations, local committees, and voluntary groups for a wide range of purposes, from schools to roads. They didn't wait for kings or parliaments to act—they *did*.

That same theme was central to what I wrote in the previous chapter on freedom and personal responsibility. Freedom isn't sustained by law alone; it's sustained by the daily choices of its citizens. Tocqueville saw that self-initiated action—the instinct to solve problems locally rather than demand permission from above—was democracy's true safeguard. It allowed ordinary people to self-correct before the collapse set in. The connection to *Good to Great* is unmistakable: progress depends on individuals who take ownership, accept reality, and move forward with disciplined resolve.

Taken together, these three perspectives—Acemoglu and Robinson's *Why Nations Fail,* Tocqueville's *Democracy in America,* and Collins' *Good to Great*—reveal a single timeless pattern: those who endure chaos don't rely on luck, laws, or slogans. They rely on discipline, accountability, and initiative.

Gen X learned that lesson firsthand. We grew up in the shadow of broken promises—the pension plans that disappeared, the tech bubbles that burst, the industries that outsourced entire generations of workers. We learned not to wait for rescue but to build resilience brick by brick. Many of us became pragmatic idealists—still believing in progress but only the kind earned through work, patience, and adjustment.

If *Why Nations Fail* showed us why systems decay, *Good to Great* showed us how individuals and organizations can break that cycle. Its "Level 5 Leadership" principle—humility paired with fierce resolve—became the modern embodiment of Tocqueville's civic virtue. It's the quiet strength of those who lead not for applause but for purpose. It's the same trait that allows a company, a nation, or an individual to reinvent themselves without losing their moral compass.

That, ultimately, is the Gen X story: we learned to balance realism with resilience, skepticism with persistence. We didn't expect life to be fair; we expected it to be hard—and we prepared accordingly. We're the bridge generation between stability and uncertainty, the analog-to-digital translators who learned that survival isn't about clinging to what worked yesterday but about mastering the art of steady reinvention.

In a world obsessed with disruption, Gen X became quietly good at endurance. We learned that greatness isn't a single act—it's a habit. And when everything else fails, the disciplined adaptability to keep moving forward is what separates those who crumble from those who build what comes next.

When I talk with members of Gen Z, I see both the best and the most uncertain parts of our future reflected back. They're the first true digital natives—born into a world already connected, cloud-based, and algorithmically tuned. Yet beneath their fluency with technology lies the same timeless tension every generation before them has faced: how to harness change without being consumed by it.

For Gen X, disruption was something that *happened* to us. The internet arrived, jobs disappeared overseas, and industries that had existed for a century collapsed in a decade. We didn't have the luxury of choosing whether to adapt; survival demanded it. Gen Z, by contrast, was *born into* a world of disruption. They've never known a world that stands still. Their challenge isn't simply surviving a sudden shift—it's building identity, resilience, and purpose in a state of constant motion.

That difference matters. Gen X learned adaptation through scarcity and hard knocks; Gen Z is learning it through abundance and information overload. Both paths require discipline—but of different kinds. We had to develop endurance; they must cultivate focus. We had to learn how to start over after failure; they have to learn how to filter truth from noise in a world overflowing with data. And in both cases, progress depends on resilience—the ability to "embrace the suck," as the military calls it. It's the willingness to face discomfort without losing direction. The

Gen X version of that came through layoffs, economic recessions, and rebuilding careers from scratch. For Gen Z, it means pushing through digital fatigue, uncertainty, and the temptation to retreat from challenge into distraction.

Nowhere is this tension more visible than in the conversation around artificial intelligence. I hear Gen Zers express equal parts excitement and anxiety about AI—how it might automate their jobs, redefine creativity, or even make human effort obsolete. But history tells us this is not a new story. Every major leap in human progress has carried the same fear.

In "*Why Nations Fail*," Acemoglu and Robinson describe how societies that fear "creative destruction" often attempt to suppress it. The Roman elite resisted water-powered mills because they threatened the slave labor system that preserved their wealth. Centuries later, Queen Elizabeth I denied inventor William Lee a patent for his mechanical knitting frame, fearing it would "tend to the ruin of many poor people." In both cases, fear of innovation froze progress.

And yet, England's story didn't end there. By the 18th century, the same nation that once stifled invention had become the epicenter of the Industrial Revolution. What changed wasn't the land or the climate—it was the mindset of its people. As political and economic freedoms expanded, so did the right to innovate. Ordinary citizens could patent ideas, invest in ventures, and profit from their ingenuity. In other words, England shifted from an *extractive* system—where elites controlled opportunity—to an *inclusive* one that rewarded creativity. That change unleashed a wave of invention that reshaped the world.

Contrast that with the Ottoman Empire and Imperial China. Both had periods of immense scientific and cultural achievement, yet both ultimately declined because their leaders chose isolation over adaptation. The Ottomans restricted printing presses for centuries to protect calligraphers and religious authorities. China turned inward, banning maritime exploration and limiting trade under the

Ming and Qing dynasties. Like the Romans before them, these empires clung to control instead of change—and paid the price.

History's lesson is unmistakable: when people are free to create, societies thrive; when they fear or forbid change, decline is inevitable. The same truth applies to individuals. Those who treat new tools as threats fall behind; those who adapt, refine, and integrate them rise.

This is where *Democracy in America* provides a perfect bridge. Tocqueville observed that America's strength lay not in its government but in its people—their initiative, community spirit, and work ethic. Citizens didn't wait for permission to solve problems; they rolled up their sleeves and got it done. That same ethic applies today. Technology may accelerate what we do, but it can't replace *how* we do it—the discipline to work hard, think critically, and act with purpose.

In "*Good to Great*," Jim Collins refers to this combination as "Level 5 Leadership"—a blend of humility and fierce resolve. The best leaders aren't those chasing headlines or trends; they're the ones quietly turning the Flywheel, doing the hard, often unglamorous work that compounds over time. That principle holds just as true for individuals and generations. The people who thrive in the AI era will be those who apply an old-fashioned work ethic to new-age tools—who use technology to amplify effort, not replace it.

This is also where personal responsibility comes in. No government, company, or algorithm will make you resilient. As Tocqueville saw, democracy depends on citizens willing to govern themselves. Likewise, success in the digital age depends on self-leadership—the discipline to manage your time, energy, and attention. Gen X learned this out of necessity; Gen Z must choose it intentionally. They live in a world that offers infinite options but little structure. Without self-imposed limits and priorities, opportunity turns into chaos.

And then there's critical thinking—the survival skill of our time. In an age of deepfakes, misinformation, and algorithmic echo chambers, discernment is the new literacy. Moving past fear means asking better questions: What's real? What's useful? What matters? Gen Z's most significant advantage is access to information; their greatest danger is being overwhelmed by it. The solution isn't retreat—it's responsibility. Learn to think deeply, to pause before reacting, to verify before believing. In short, *use* technology, but don't let it use you.

That's where Gen X and Gen Z meet—in the shared need for *disciplined adaptability.* We learned it through rebuilding; they'll learn it through refining. For us, it meant accepting that no career or institution was permanent. For them, it will mean realizing that no algorithm or platform can define who they are. Progress always begins at the same place: when individuals take ownership of change instead of waiting for someone else to manage it.

If Gen X were the bridge generation, Gen Z is the next foundation. They stand at the start of a century where AI will touch everything from how we work to how we think. The question isn't whether AI will replace people—it's whether people will rise to redefine what *human* means in an age of machines. The advantage goes to those who keep their curiosity alive, maintain a sharp work ethic, and preserve their sense of purpose.

In that sense, Gen Z's challenge mirrors ours: to build something better amid uncertainty, to find freedom in responsibility, and to turn disruption into discipline. The tools have changed, but the formula remains the same. Greatness—whether for nations, companies, or individuals—still comes from the same place: the courage to adapt, the humility to learn, and the steady resolve to keep moving forward.

If history teaches us that adaptability determines survival, then the challenge for Gen Z is to make adaptability a daily habit—not just a reaction when things go wrong. Resilience isn't luck or optimism; it's a discipline. It's built through choices repeated over time—routines that train the mind to stay steady while the world keeps shifting.

Jim Collins referred to this as *"the Flywheel Effect"* in *Good to Great*, the concept that greatness doesn't arrive in a single breakthrough moment but rather through hundreds of small, consistent pushes in the same direction. Companies like **Walgreens** and **Nucor Steel**, which Collins studied, didn't leap from mediocrity to excellence overnight. They identified what they did best, aligned around it, and improved one turn at a time—building unstoppable momentum while competitors chased shortcuts.

That same principle works for people. If you want to thrive through disruption—whether it's AI, economic instability, or social upheaval—build your own flywheel. Pick the skills that matter most in your field, improve them incrementally every day, and protect the integrity of your habits. Progress won't feel dramatic, but it compounds over time. The danger isn't failure—it's distraction.

1. Start with Your Hedgehog Concept: Find the Intersection of Purpose, Talent, and Opportunity

Collins wrote that great organizations find what they can be *the best in the world at*, what drives their economic engine, and what they're deeply passionate about. The same applies to individuals. Gen Z lives in a world overflowing with options, but clarity comes from convergence. Ask yourself three questions:

1. What am I naturally good at or drawn to?
2. What problems do I genuinely care about solving?
3. What will the world still pay for—or need—ten years from now?

Your personal "hedgehog" lies at the intersection. Once you find it, stop chasing everything else. That focus is what keeps you grounded when technology advances faster than you can keep up with.

I remember the wise professor advising us to, "*...just add knowledge to the world.*" That meant that what I was doing didn't have to be earth-shaking. It didn't have to be a homerun. It just had to be new. I needed to get on base. Begin small, build credibility, and gather a foothold. For me, that meant becoming the leading expert in instructional analysis and design within the Space Force. I started in a one-deep position, expanded it to a six-person team, and now manage operations for over 130 people working across the education, training, modeling, and simulation industry. Like Collins' flywheel, each small turn of effort built the next opportunity.

2. Confront the Brutal Facts —but Never Lose Faith

Collins calls this the *Stockdale Paradox,* named after Admiral James Stockdale, who survived years of torture in Vietnam by balancing two truths: unshakable faith that he would prevail and brutal honesty about the present reality.

Gen Z faces its own paradox—you must believe in your future while confronting the world as it is: volatile, expensive, and uncertain. AI will change the job market. Automation will replace routine work. But instead of denying those realities, face them head-on. Learn what machines do better, then master what they can't: creativity, judgment, empathy, persuasion, and leadership.

Try this thought experiment. Imagine you're a factory assembly-line worker in the auto industry as robots arrive on the floor. The 1980s and 1990s saw exactly that—automation transforming Detroit's plants. Many workers feared extinction. Some quit in frustration. Others retrained to operate and maintain the very machines that replaced them. Entire industries restructured, but the world didn't end. Cars got cheaper, safer, and more efficient; new jobs emerged in robotics, design, and logistics. The lesson: *when disruption comes, don't freeze—reposition.* Every era has its reset; those who stay curious find their place in the new order.

3. Build a Work Ethic that Outlasts Technology

Tocqueville admired early Americans for their habit of *doing.* They formed committees, built schools, and fixed roads without waiting for orders. They adopted the *"No one is coming to help*" philosophy. That civic reflex—the belief that work itself carries dignity—is the antidote to helplessness. In the digital age, it's easy to confuse activity with accomplishment: scrolling, posting, reacting. Real work leaves the world tangibly better at the end of the day.

AI can process information, but it can't *care.* It can generate text, but it can't sacrifice comfort for excellence. The most irreplaceable people will be those who work not because they must, but because they choose to *build.*

Now apply that to the worker who's adopted "quiet quitting" as a philosophy—doing the bare minimum and waiting for AI to shoulder the rest. I understand the fantasy: machines doing the work while you relax and create. But that was never reality. There must be *value* in the exchange. Be the *added-value* part of AI—the human insight, discipline, and initiative the algorithm lacks. Technology amplifies purpose; it doesn't replace it.

4. Embrace the Suck—Then Extract the Lesson

Resilience isn't built in comfort zones. Gen X learned this through layoffs, recessions, and reinvention. Every generation faces a trial by fire; AI and automation will be yours. When a project collapses or an algorithm makes your skills obsolete, don't look away—study the failure.

In *Good to Great,* Collins describes how **Nucor Steel**, once near bankruptcy, reinvented itself through innovation and culture. Workers shared profits; hierarchies flattened. Nucor described its hiring practice of bringing on six people to do the work of ten and paying them as if they were eight. This system rewarded efficiency while preserving pride. Everyone gained because everyone contributed.

I recall recently suggesting something similar while advising local school board candidates. I proposed tackling the teacher shortage by integrating asynchronous learning, intelligent tutors, and AI-guided lessons—reducing costs while improving outcomes. The idea wasn't popular; it challenged tradition. But innovation often feels like heresy before it becomes common sense. Education, like any industry, must evolve to survive—the only question is *who leads that evolution.* Those willing to endure criticism and discomfort to make progress will own the future.

5. Practice Disciplined Adaptability

Collins found that great companies were paradoxical: they held firm to core values while constantly experimenting with methods. Gen Z can apply the same logic. Know your principles—integrity, curiosity, perseverance—but stay flexible in how you apply them.

Why Nations Fail offers a powerful example in the post-colonial trajectories of **Botswana** and **Sierra Leone.** Both nations began their independence with poverty, limited infrastructure, and fragile political systems. Yet Botswana charted a different path—building *inclusive institutions* grounded in property rights, accountability, and long-term planning. Its leaders established transparent systems of governance, encouraged open trade, and reinvested national wealth from diamond mining into education and public infrastructure. Sierra Leone, by contrast, fell into *extractive politics*. In this system, power is concentrated among elites, corruption replaces accountability, and national resources serve a few instead of the many. The difference wasn't in geography, ethnicity, or resources; it was **in discipline**—the discipline to adapt without abandoning one's principles. Botswana modernized while remaining accountable, demonstrating that values and evolution can coexist.

We see echoes of that same struggle here in the United States today. There are groups and institutions—public and private alike—that cling to power under the banner of *safety* or *security,* expanding rules and requirements that restrict individual decision-making in the name of protection. These efforts often begin with good intentions but drift toward *extractive control*—systems that limit innovation, personal responsibility, and freedom of choice. It's the same trap that *Why Nations Fail* warns about: when institutions become overly intrinsic—serving those in power rather than the people—they lose adaptability. The strength of any nation, organization, or generation depends on keeping its systems *extrinsic*—focused outward, empowering individuals to act, innovate, and hold leadership accountable. The moment we prioritize control over creativity, or regulation over initiative, we begin the slow decline that history has repeatedly documented.

Think of adaptability as a muscle. Each time you master a new tool, adjust a habit, or accept feedback, you strengthen it. The goal isn't to avoid uncertainty—it's to grow comfortable inside it.

6. Protect Your Attention Like a Strategic Asset

In a world designed to steal your focus, attention is power. The average Gen Z adult consumes between six and ten hours of digital content daily.[6] But as Collins said, *"If you have more than three priorities, you have none."*

Tocqueville saw the same principle two centuries ago. He warned that democratic citizens could drown in trivial distractions—what he called the "petty amusements" of comfort and consumption. Today's social media feeds are the modern equivalent. Choose your inputs deliberately. Read deeply and invest in non-fiction books. Study the mechanics behind success, not just the highlight reels.

In *Good to Great*, Collins noted that great leaders maintained a "stop doing" list alongside their "to-do" list. They cut noise to preserve focus. You can do the same: prune your digital diet. Every minute of attention is a vote for the person you're becoming.

7. Turn Fear into Curiosity

The most successful nations, *Why Nations Fail* reminds us, are those that view disruption as an opportunity, not a danger. When England embraced industrial innovation, it surged ahead; when the Ottoman Empire and China turned inward, they stagnated.

Curiosity is the antidote to fear. When faced with uncertainty, ask, *'What can I learn here that others overlook?'* That's how innovators are born. In *Democracy in America*, Tocqueville marveled that Americans "improvise" solutions faster than any people he'd seen—not because they lacked fear, but because curiosity overpowered it. In *Good to Great*, Collins found that transformative leaders were relentlessly curious—constantly asking questions, running experiments, and learning from failure. Fear paralyzes; curiosity moves.

8. Lead Yourself Before You Try to Lead Others

Leadership isn't a title; it's a matter of consistency. Collins' *Level 5 Leaders* were humble yet relentless. They didn't chase attention—they pursued excellence. You can do the same: keep your promises, show up on time, and finish what you start.

In *Why Nations Fail*, inclusive societies thrived because their leaders built systems, not cults of personality. In *Democracy in America*, Tocqueville found that American leadership was distributed—citizens led themselves through local action before leading others. Authentic leadership begins within.

Start small. Lead your own habits, your learning, your work ethic. When you can manage yourself, you're ready to influence others. In a world where visibility often outweighs substance, consistency will always win.

Greatness—whether in a company, a nation, or a generation—is never granted; it's earned through disciplined adaptability. Gen X learned it through hardship; Gen Z must choose it amid abundance. The tools have changed, but the principles haven't:

- **Confront reality without cynicism.**
- **Work hard even when no one's watching.**
- **Stay curious, but stay grounded.**
- **Adapt quickly, but with purpose.**

The future won't belong to those who fear the machines—it will belong to those who think, build, and lead with integrity in spite of them.

The same timeless pattern runs through every story from *Why Nations Fail*, *Democracy in America*, and *Good to Great*: success favors those who combine courage with discipline, innovation with virtue, and change with accountability. Gen Z now holds that torch. The question isn't whether they can handle disruption—it's whether they can build something enduring from it.

The rise of any person, organization, or nation begins with the courage to adapt and the discipline to stay accountable.

Progress has always belonged to those who move toward disruption, not away from it. Whether in business, government, or personal life, the difference between those who rise and those who collapse isn't strength or intelligence — it's adaptability.

Ronald Reagan reminded us that *"freedom is never more than one generation away from extinction."* What he meant applies equally to progress itself: no generation inherits success or relevance automatically. Both must be renewed through effort — through innovation, accountability, and the willingness to embrace change instead of fearing it.

History, experience, and data all point to the same truth: when systems or individuals cling to comfort and resist transformation, decline follows. When they adapt, experiment, and hold themselves accountable, renewal begins. That idea sits at the heart of the three works that shaped my understanding of how people, institutions, and nations move from good to great — and why some never make it.

The Warning from History – *Why Nations Fail*

In *Why Nations Fail*, Daron Acemoglu and James Robinson demonstrate that societies collapse not because of bad luck or geography, but because their institutions lose **inclusivity** — the ability to empower innovation rather than suppress it. When power consolidates in "extractive" systems that protect the status quo, creativity suffocates. Progress slows. The system decays.

But inclusive systems — those that encourage experimentation, reward accountability, and distribute opportunity — unleash human potential. They transform uncertainty into invention.

That same pattern exists in business, community, and personal life. When we resist change, hide from risk, or cling to old routines, we build our own extractive systems — internal ones that trade growth for safety. But when we embrace disruption with curiosity and courage, we evolve.

Thriving nations, like thriving individuals, are not the most comfortable — they're the most **adaptable**. Innovation and accountability, not fear and complacency, are the engines of renewal.

The Strength of the Citizen – *Democracy in America*

Alexis de Tocqueville saw this truth in motion long before the Industrial Age or the Internet. When he traveled through 1830s America, he was astonished not by its wealth but by its **participation**. Americans didn't wait for orders or permission; they formed committees, built schools, and tackled problems directly. This culture of voluntary association made democracy resilient because it made change a collective effort.

That insight still holds. Systems that depend entirely on leadership collapse when leaders fail. Systems that rely on citizens — or employees, or team members — endure. When ordinary people step forward to shape what's next, no disruption is too large.

I witnessed this firsthand when I joined my local caucus. I wasn't out to change the world; I just wanted to understand it better. But that small step forced me to choose — not between parties, but between values, ideas, and people who represented them. In rooms of only a few hundred, sometimes fewer, we were deciding who would appear on the larger ballot. I realized democracy doesn't die from corruption alone; it withers from apathy. Participation is not just a right — it's a renewable resource.

Tocqueville's timeless message: Institutions endure only when their citizens evolve in tandem with them.

The Discipline of Greatness – *Good to Great*

Jim Collins' *Good to Great* isn't a business book about success — it's a study of transformation. Collins found that great organizations share a single trait: **disciplined adaptation**. They face disruptive technology, economic shifts, or internal crises not with panic, but with methodical innovation. Their leaders confront hard truths, take responsibility, and keep turning what Collins called the "flywheel" — small, consistent actions that build unstoppable momentum over time.

That principle applies everywhere. Progress doesn't come from avoiding chaos; it comes from learning how to use it. The same disruption that topples one company can launch another. The same technology that replaces jobs can create new industries — if people have the courage and discipline to evolve with it.

Greatness, in short, isn't about predicting the future; it's about preparing for it.

Bringing It All Together

If *Why Nations Fail* warns about what happens when systems fear change, *Democracy in America* shows how participation keeps them alive, and *Good to Great* explains how disciplined innovation makes them endure. Together, they form a blueprint for how individuals, organizations, and nations can rise — and rise again — in a world that never stops changing.

- **Encourage inclusion and accountability** — innovation dies in closed systems.
- **Engage locally and think globally** — transformation starts where you stand.
- **Stay disciplined through disruption** — consistency is the antidote to chaos.

I've seen these lessons play out in my own life. From financial collapse to renewal, from passivity to civic engagement, the pattern remains the same: adaptability brings opportunity; responsibility sustains it.

So here's the call to action for every reader — Gen X, Gen Z, and anyone in between:

- Don't fear disruption; **study it.**
- Don't resist change; **shape it.**
- Don't wait for systems to fix themselves; **lead by example.**

Because innovation without accountability becomes chaos, and accountability without innovation becomes decay. The balance of both is where progress—and freedom—lives.

If there's one message I'd pass forward, it's this:

Rise doesn't come from strength; it comes from motion.

Nations, companies, and people endure not by standing still, but by continuously becoming better than they were yesterday.

---

[1] *Financial Times*, "Americans Are Reading Less for Pleasure—Even as Publishing Booms," Aug 18 2023; *The Guardian*, "Reading for Pleasure in the U.S. Falls by Over 40 Percent Since Early 2000s," Aug 20 2023; *University of Florida News*, "Study Finds Americans Reading Less Each Year Despite Growth in Online Content," Sept 2023. Based on U.S. Bureau of Labor Statistics *American Time Use Survey* (2003–2023).

[2] *National Endowment for the Arts*, "Federal Data on Reading for Pleasure: All Signs Show a Slump," *NEA Arts Blog*, Jan 2024. Derived from *Survey of Public Participation in the Arts* (2017–2022).

[3] *Encyclopedia Britannica*, "1824 Constitution of Mexico," updated 2024; *Wikipedia*, "1824 Constitution of Mexico," last modified Sept 2024, https://en.wikipedia.org/wiki/1824_Constitution_of_Mexico.

[4] *Bullock Texas State History Museum*, "Project Constitution: The Republic of Mexico," Texas State Preservation Board, 2023, https://www.thestoryoftexas.com/discover/artifacts/project-constitution-republic-of-mexico.

[5] William Lee's mechanical knitting frame (invented 1589) was denied a patent by Queen Elizabeth I, who feared the invention would cause unemployment among manual knitters. The patent was later approved under James I, helping to spark England's textile mechanization. See: Acemoglu & Robinson, *Why Nations Fail* (2012), Ch. 7; Encyclopædia Britannica, "William Lee – English Inventor."

[6] Talker Research, *Media Consumption Trend Report* (2024), Gen Z consumes ~6.6 hours/day. talkerresearch.com; UK Adobe / media survey cited by Bobble Digital, "Gen Z are spending 10.6 hours consuming content" Bobble Digital; CTAM, *The State of Gen Z – Media Behaviors and Industry Trends*, "on average, Gen Z spends about 6 hours and 40 minutes online each day."

Chapter 12: Faith, Religion, and the Search for Purpose

How belief—in God, in principle, and in something larger than ourselves—shapes the moral compass that gives both individuals and nations their purpose.

In the last chapter, I discussed how individuals, systems, and even nations rise when they learn to embrace change and accountability rather than fear or complacency. This chapter continues that thread by exploring the deeper foundation that sustains those qualities—faith. Over the years, I've drawn from many thinkers who helped shape my understanding of what it means to live with purpose. I didn't come to their insights through church pews or Sunday sermons, but through the long road of experience—decades of reading, failing, reflecting, and growing.

Like the previous chapter, this one builds upon the ideas of authors who've profoundly influenced my thinking: **M. Scott Peck**, whose *The Road Less Traveled* and *Further Along the Road Less Traveled* taught me that spiritual growth begins with honesty and discipline; **Rick Warren**, whose *The Purpose Driven Life* reframed my understanding of meaning and service; and **John Locke**, whose writings on liberty, faith, and moral responsibility helped anchor an entire nation's conscience. Together, they form the framework for this discussion—not as religious doctrine, but as a practical philosophy of purpose.

Much of what follows comes from a man in his late fifties, hardened by life and thankful for its blessings. Not an adolescent trying to make a name for himself or a father and husband trying to provide materialistic things for his family. The truth is, I wasn't particularly religious growing up—and understandably so. I was born into a Methodist-leaning family; my great-grandfather on my maternal grandmother's side was one of the founding members of the Methodist Church in Morgan Hill, California. Yet, except for weddings, funerals, or the occasional Easter service, my parents never took me to church. Like most families, religion, money, and politics were considered topics best left alone. Why? I'm still not sure.

At nine years old, my life took a sharp turn when my mother remarried and moved us to rural Oklahoma—right in the heart of the Bible Belt. That's where I first encountered religion, though not necessarily for the right reasons. In middle school, I had a crush on a girl who attended the local church youth program, so naturally, I started going too. She stopped going after a few weeks, but by then I'd made new friends—and there was the added incentive of a promised trip to Silver Dollar City in Branson if I kept showing up. So, I did.

Later in high school, I learned that faith in small-town Oklahoma came with its own peculiar sales pitches. Evangelical revivals promised salvation, community, and—on more than one occasion—the attention of a pretty girl. I can still picture myself sitting through those fiery sermons about sin and redemption, the preacher shouting, "Come forward if you want to be saved!" I'd glance at the girl next to me, and I knew exactly what was expected. Up I went, received my redemption, and afterward, there was free pizza and soda—and maybe a make-out session in my pickup truck with the pretty girl who brought me. After all, I was now "saved" because of her.

Looking back, the hypocrisy was hard to miss. The same preachers who railed against sin on Sunday were sometimes the ones caught in scandal by Wednesday. I heard stories of Baptist pastors running off with other men's wives, or of their families struggling behind closed doors—alcoholism, addiction, and worse. By the time I reached college, studying engineering and later physics, I had no patience for what I saw as moral theatrics. I wasn't about to surrender my reason to what I then viewed as superstition about some "invisible man in the sky."

Still, I couldn't quite commit to atheism either. Its arguments struck me as shallow as the fire-and-brimstone preaching I'd rejected. So, I became an agnostic—a man hedging his bets. I told myself that if God existed, He'd need to show me proof. Like C.S. Lewis once said, I was "the most reluctant convert." What I didn't realize at the time was that my skepticism wasn't protecting me—it was limiting me. By refusing to believe in anything greater than myself, I was also cutting myself off from one of life's most significant sources of purpose: faith.

If freedom gives us room to choose, then faith provides us with a reason to do so. A nation—or a person—without a sense of higher purpose eventually loses direction, mistaking movement for progress and comfort for meaning. That's the quiet danger of the modern age: we've learned to master the mechanics of life but forgotten how to ask *why* we're living it.

Scott Peck opened his classic *The Road Less Traveled* with a line that startled readers in its simplicity:

"Life is difficult. Once we truly see this truth… we transcend it."

He wasn't preaching pessimism; he was reminding us that meaning begins with acceptance. Life's hardships aren't punishment—they're invitations to grow. Peck, a psychiatrist who fused psychology and spirituality, believed that discipline, responsibility, and love were the tools by which humans mature their souls. Faith, in his view, was less about believing the unbelievable and more about committing to truth, wherever it leads. "The journey of spiritual growth," he wrote later, "is a journey of becoming an increasingly better lover of reality."

That idea—of facing reality instead of escaping it—defined much of the Gen X experience. We grew up watching institutions falter, seeing hypocrisy in pulpits and politics alike, yet still sensing that something sacred had to exist beyond the chaos. Faith, for us, became quieter but no less real. It was found in the late-night prayer whispered before a deployment, in the decision to stay faithful when walking away would have been easier, or in the determination to raise children with values even when the world mocked them.

Rick Warren, in *The Purpose Driven Life*, offered a framework that seemed tailor-made for that struggle. His opening sentence became one of the most-quoted lines in modern spiritual writing:

"It's not about you."

That one sentence cuts directly against the current of self-promotion that floods our culture and many of the new-age churches that want to appeal to the masses by watering down their foundational beliefs. Warren reminds us that purpose doesn't come from looking inward at what we want, but upward at what we're called to do. "You were made by God and for God," he writes, "and until you understand that, life will never make sense."

It's a bold statement in an age that glorifies self-definition. Yet, it echoes something America's founders knew centuries earlier—that liberty without virtue quickly devours itself.

John Locke, whose writings inspired Jefferson and Madison, declared in his *Second Treatise of Government*:

"Men being all the workmanship of one omnipotent and infinitely wise Maker… they are His property, whose workmanship they are."

Locke wasn't preaching theology; he was laying the philosophical groundwork for self-government. If our rights come from God, they cannot be taken by kings or congresses. But that truth carries responsibility: if liberty is a gift from the divine, then how we use it becomes a moral test. The founders understood that no system of laws could long protect a people who had lost their internal compass. As John Adams later warned, "Our Constitution was made only for a moral and religious people. It is wholly inadequate to the government of any other."

The connection between these voices—Peck, Warren, and Locke—spans centuries yet points to the same truth: belief, when rightly held, disciplines the soul. It transforms freedom from indulgence into stewardship.

Faith is not blind obedience; it's the courage to walk "the road less traveled," trusting that truth and goodness still lead somewhere worth going. And if that's true for a single person, it's equally valid for a nation.

As we'll see throughout this chapter, every generation must rediscover that road for itself. For Gen Z, the challenge isn't whether God exists, but whether meaning does—and how to build a life that answers that question with both conviction and compassion.

Gen X has always lived between worlds. We were raised by the last generation that viewed church as routine and came of age in the first era that questioned everything. We grew up watching the fall of heroes—preachers caught in scandals, politicians caught in lies, corporations caught cheating the very people who built them. Somewhere between the televangelist and the cynic, we learned to keep our faith private.

For many of us, faith became something deeply personal but rarely spoken aloud. We learned early that belief and hypocrisy often walked hand in hand, so we kept a cautious distance. But underneath that guardedness, something else was happening: we were quietly searching for meaning that could survive disillusionment. We didn't need more sermons;

we needed integrity—something tangible enough to withstand the weight of adulthood, disappointment, and loss.

Scott Peck described that process perfectly in *The Road Less Traveled*. He wrote, “Discipline is the basic set of tools we require to solve life’s problems.”

To Peck, discipline wasn’t punishment—it was love translated into action. His message resonated with a generation that learned to measure faith not by what people said on Sunday, but by what they did on Monday. Many of us didn’t find God through a sermon, but through experience: the birth of a child, the death of a friend, or the quiet moments when logic failed and humility filled the gap. Peck’s insight that “life is a series of problems” and that growth requires the willingness to confront them head-on became, for Gen X, a kind of unspoken creed.

In that sense, our faith grew backward. We didn’t start with belief and drift into doubt—we began with doubt and worked our way toward something we could believe in. It wasn’t religion that changed us; it was responsibility. We got jobs, families, and mortgages, and suddenly abstract questions about purpose turned painfully practical. Faith began to take root, not as a ritual, but as resilience—the ability to do the right thing even when no one was watching.

I didn’t start to take my faith seriously until I was married and preparing to have children. Like most of my generation, my conversion wasn’t dramatic—it was gradual. I had begun to notice a strange pattern: some of the greatest minds in human history—men like **Isaac Newton**, who wrote extensively on theology; **Blaise Pascal**, the mathematician and philosopher who said, “The heart has its reasons which reason does not know”; **Francis Collins**, who led the Human Genome Project and yet wrote *The Language of God*; **Søren Kierkegaard**, the father of existential philosophy; **C.S. Lewis**, who moved from atheism to faith; and even **Leonardo da Vinci**, whose art and invention carried traces of divine fascination—all of them saw no contradiction between reason and belief. What did these men know that I didn’t?

That question sent me down an unexpected road. Around that same time, I started listening to **Dr. Laura Schlessinger's** radio program. She was controversial, often abrasive, and far from perfect, but what caught my attention wasn't her tone—it was her conviction. While the world was growing louder about self-expression and "living your truth," Dr. Laura spoke about **moral obligation, discipline, and personal accountability**. She reminded listeners that morality isn't situational—it's chosen. Her show reinforced something I'd later find echoed in Peck's and Warren's writing: that love without responsibility is indulgence, and freedom without morality is chaos.

One day, she took a call from a couple asking how to raise their children when each parent came from a different religious background. The situation and follow-on advice prompted me to realize that I needed to address my own moral questions not for my sake, but for the sake of my future children. That reality hit me harder than any sermon I'd heard. Preparing to become a father myself, I realized that my hang-ups about organized religion were insignificant compared to my responsibility to raise my children with a moral compass. It was the moment I began to see faith not as something I needed to prove, but something I needed to practice—for the sake of others, not myself.

Not having been tied to any church, I began looking for a place where I could anchor that belief. I'd been married in the **Catholic Church**, and my father-in-law, Joe, was deeply connected to his faith, so I started there. I met **Father Pete**, the military chaplain at Minot AFB, and spent a year studying Catholicism under his guidance. Father Pete was unlike any priest I'd ever met—he was patient, humble, and surprisingly open to questioning. He also happened to be a fan of Scott Peck. That shared respect broke the ice. We had long conversations about discipline, love, and the purpose of suffering. He encouraged me to challenge doctrine and make my faith my own.

I also came to understand something important: there's a vast difference between those who were **born into religion** and carry its guilt and expectations, and those who **choose faith** after living without it. I wasn't a "recovering Catholic." I was a man making an independent decision to believe.

A decade later, facing divorce, I turned back to that same church for guidance—and it was there for me. The irony is that after our separation, it was my Catholic wife who drifted toward atheism, leaving me to raise our boys within the faith. It wasn't about dogma; it was about providing them the structure I'd lacked.

When my youngest son was confirmed—the third of three—I remember standing beside him as his grandfather Joe, my ex-father-in-law, proudly watched. Even after the divorce, Joe and I remained close. We shared an understanding that faith wasn't about perfection; it was about perseverance. We both believed it was my duty to make sure the boys grew up with a moral foundation stronger than the one I'd been given. Joe passed not long after that, but the bond remained. To this day, my sons still talk about him with reverence. They occasionally ask to attend Mass—not out of obligation, but out of respect for their grandfather's memory. And though I encourage them to find their own path when it comes to faith, I cherish those moments when they choose to walk beside me into the pews.

For me, faith wasn't superstition—it became structure. It was the invisible framework that gave meaning to hard work, love, and sacrifice. The same discipline that Peck called "the tool of love" and Warren called "living on purpose" began showing up everywhere: in how I treated people, how I raised my children, and how I led others.

We didn't return to religion because we needed comfort; we returned because we needed accountability—to something higher than our own opinions. That shift marked the quiet transformation of an entire generation. We didn't find our purpose in loud declarations or emotional revivals, but in the steady rhythm of responsibility: showing up, doing the work, and keeping our word.

Peck's reminder that "Love is the will to extend oneself for the purpose of nurturing one's own or another's spiritual growth" became more than a quote—it became a definition of maturity. We learned that love isn't just emotion—it's effort. Faith, in that same sense, became effort too. It was choosing to believe that life's difficulties were not barriers but pathways, that discipline was a form of grace, and that service to others was the surest way to stay grounded in something eternal.

So, while the world saw a generation drifting from organized religion, what was really happening was far more subtle. Gen X was redefining what belief looked like. We stripped away the performance and held onto the principles. We turned skepticism into discernment, rebellion into responsibility, and religion into relationship.

By the time many of us reached middle age, we began to understand what **Locke**, **Peck**, and **Warren** were each saying in their own ways—that **faith and freedom are inseparable**. One disciplines the other. Freedom without belief collapses into chaos, and belief without responsibility hardens into hypocrisy. The sweet spot lies in the middle: a faith grounded enough to endure, humble enough to question, and active enough to serve.

That balance—between independence and surrender, skepticism and trust—is what ultimately shaped our moral grounding. And it's the legacy we now have a chance to pass on.

Every generation inherits both the questions and the consequences of the one before it. For Gen X, our search for faith began with skepticism—we needed to see integrity before we could believe in it. For Gen Z, the journey often starts from a different place. They were raised in a world where information is instant, identities are fluid, and institutions—from religion to government to media—have lost much of their authority. Yet, for all the noise, this generation is quietly asking the same timeless questions: *Who am I? Why am I here? What gives life meaning?*

In that sense, Gen X and Gen Z are not opposites—they're mirror images separated by technology. Where we learned to distrust authority after it failed us, Gen Z was born into a world where authority often feels absent or hollow. They grew up in a digital wilderness with unlimited information and almost no consensus on what was true. While we questioned the church, they now question everything—politics, media, identity, even belief itself. And yet, amid all that questioning, a familiar hunger remains: the search for purpose.

The difference lies in how each generation pursues it. Gen X sought meaning through endurance—through building, providing, surviving, and slowly discovering faith in the process. Gen Z seeks meaning through **authenticity**—encompassing connection, integrity, and a sense of belonging. They are less interested in what people believe and more interested in *whether they live it honestly.* In that sense, they've taken our skepticism and evolved it into discernment.

Rick Warren's message in *The Purpose Driven Life*—that "It's not about you"—feels almost countercultural in a generation raised on personal branding, self-promotion, and curated identity. Yet beneath the surface, Gen Z is beginning to rediscover what he meant. Many are drawn to causes larger than themselves—mental health, climate justice, social equity—not because they reject meaning, but because they yearn for it. What they often lack is the moral foundation to sustain that passion without collapsing into burnout or cynicism.

This is where our generations converge. Gen X learned that discipline and service give faith endurance. Gen Z is learning that passion without principle can quickly devolve into restlessness. Their challenge isn't apathy—it's fragmentation.

Many of them care deeply about many causes, but without a spiritual anchor, caring can feel like drowning.

Scott Peck would have recognized their struggle. He taught: "We must be willing to suffer through the pains of growth in order to reach a higher level of consciousness."

That "higher level" doesn't come through comfort or constant validation—it comes through discipline, through a willingness to confront the inconvenient truth rather than evade it. Gen Z senses that pull; they just express it differently. Instead of pews, they find community through podcasts, online discussion groups, volunteer networks, and shared experiential projects. Instead of sermons, they listen to mentors. Instead of dogma, they seek conversation.

And while many have drifted from organized religion, few have abandoned spirituality altogether. Surveys show that although Gen Z reports the lowest formal religious affiliation of any generation, they express high levels of interest in spirituality, meditation, and purpose-driven living. They may not speak the language of faith—but they are fluent in longing. They want to believe in something—they just want it to be real.

However, that trend is shifting, especially among **young men**. Data suggests that male Gen Zers are increasingly returning to religious practice in meaningful ways. For example, Barna reports that **among Gen Z men, commitment to Jesus increased by 15 percentage points between 2019 and 2025**.[1] And in broader church attendance, the "typical Gen Z churchgoer" attends **1.9 weekends per month**, slightly more frequently than Millennials.[2] Some observers see Gen Z men as leading a "religious resurgence"—not simply returning to tradition, but seeking spiritual depth on their own terms.[3]

Another revealing pattern: in many surveys, Gen Z men are now **less likely** than Gen Z women to identify as religiously unaffiliated. For instance, PRRI data finds that **39% of Gen Z women** report being unaffiliated, compared to **31% of Gen**

Z men.[4] This shift suggests that male youth are responding differently to cultural narratives about faith, purpose, and identity.

A key reason for this movement—and one that bridges generations—is the influence of thinkers like **Jordan Peterson**. His public persona, lectures, and writings have deeply resonated with many young men who feel disoriented or dismissed by modern culture. Peterson emphasizes **personal responsibility, meaning, and order**—urging men to "stand up straight," confront chaos, and take small steps toward disciplined virtue.[5] For many, he has become a de facto mentor at a time when traditional spiritual authority feels hollow.

Peterson appeals especially to young men who feel the cultural scripts around masculinity are broken or unfair. He gives them a vocabulary for purpose—not in spite of reason, but through it. Many young men see in him someone who refuses to indulge victimhood and demands accountability in a culture that often rewards passivity.[6] Critics point out that his framing can sometimes veer into controversy. Still, the underlying draw remains: meaning grounded in discipline and identity.[7]

In short, Gen X's moral evolution was forged in silence, forged through responsibility. Gen Z's rediscovery of spirituality is being forged in noise, forged through authenticity, experimentation, and the search for a personal anchor.

When I talk with my own sons, I see this clearly. They're not drawn to church for ritual—they're drawn to connection, to stories, to legacy. Their grandfather, the man they deeply loved, was well-connected to his church; it holds meaning for them because it held meaning for him. That shared memory builds bridges more quickly than doctrine ever could.

In a way, Gen Z is picking up where we left off. If Gen X rebuilt faith through responsibility, Gen Z is rebuilding it through authenticity. Both generations are pushing back against pretense, though in different ways. We stripped away the hypocrisy of institutions; they're stripping away the masks of social performance. What we called duty, they call purpose. What we saw as belief, they see as alignment.

And that may be the most significant connection between us: both generations are striving to live lives that matter. We speak different dialects of the same truth—that the human soul is wired to serve something greater than itself.

Our task now, as Gen Xers, is not to lecture but to guide—to help Gen Z understand that faith and purpose don't have to be antagonists to reason or individuality. They can coexist, just as they did for the great thinkers who came before us. Peck taught us discipline. Warren taught us design. Locke taught us responsibility. And Jordan Peterson—however imperfectly—has reintroduced the urgency of meaning in a chaotic age. Together, these voices remind both generations that **freedom without virtue is hollow, and virtue without purpose is blind.**

If Gen X's faith was forged in silence, Gen Z's may be forged in noise. But both generations are searching for the same quiet truth—that belief, when lived authentically, still has the power to change a life… and perhaps even a nation.

If the first half of life teaches us how to survive, the second half should teach us how to live with purpose. The older I get, the clearer it becomes that wisdom isn't found in comfort or control—it's found in **discipline, humility, and service**. The great thinkers who shaped my perspective—**Scott Peck, Rick Warren, John Locke, and Jordan Peterson**—all arrived at this same truth from different directions. Yet, their messages converge in a single challenge: *to live as though your life actually matters.*

Each of them offers a practical framework for doing exactly that.

Scott Peck: Discipline as Love in Action

Peck's *The Road Less Traveled* begins with a line that could summarize every life worth living:

"Life is difficult."

He didn't mean that cynically—he meant it as an invitation. To accept life's difficulty is to stop waiting for things to get easy and start becoming strong enough to meet them as they are. Peck described four tools of discipline: **delaying gratification, accepting responsibility, dedication to truth, and balancing.** Those tools aren't theoretical—they're spiritual practices.

In many ways, Peck's ideas align with what Admiral Jim Stockdale famously called the **Stockdale Paradox**—the principle that sustained him through seven years as a prisoner of war: *confront the brutal facts of your reality while never losing faith that you will prevail in the end.* In other words, life sometimes just plain sucks—**deal with it.** Don't sugarcoat the pain or wait for rescue. Have faith that there's a bigger purpose at play than just your own happiness.

To **delay gratification** is to prioritize long-term growth over short-term pleasure. To **accept responsibility** is to stop blaming others and take ownership of your life. To **dedicate yourself to truth** is to face reality, even when it's uncomfortable. And to **balance** is to keep love and duty, self and others, in tension without breaking.

Peck's advice is simple but subversive in today's culture: the road to peace runs directly through discomfort. His work reminds us that maturity is not freedom from pain—it's freedom from avoidance.

Lesson for Gen X and Gen Z: Don't mistake ease for happiness. Learn to carry weight, not because it's fun, but because it builds character—and character is what sustains faith when emotion fades.

Rick Warren: Purpose through Service

If Peck taught us to accept life's difficulty, **Rick Warren** taught us *why* we endure it. His book *The Purpose Driven Life* opens with a sentence that has humbled millions:

"It's not about you."

That may sound restrictive, but it's actually liberating. When life stops revolving around you, you become free to find where you truly belong. Warren identifies five central purposes: **worship, fellowship, discipleship, ministry, and mission**—each pointing outward, not inward.

I didn't fully embrace the role of religion until I started thinking about my future children more than I did myself. Preparing to become a father forced me to reexamine the values I wanted to pass down. Warren's framework suddenly made sense—not as theology, but as **architecture for a meaningful life.**

You don't have to share his exact faith to see the brilliance of his design. The human heart finds meaning in contribution. Whether through faith, family, mentorship, or community, service gives shape to belief. Warren's model suggests that happiness is the *by-product* of significance, and significance comes only through service.

Lesson: Purpose begins where self-interest ends. If you feel lost, stop asking *"What do I want?"* and start asking *"What am I needed for?"*

John Locke: Freedom with Moral Boundaries

Centuries before the emergence of psychology or self-help movements, **John Locke** grounded liberty itself in faith. He argued that our rights are *God-given* and therefore cannot be revoked by human institutions. But Locke's insight cuts both ways—if our rights are divine, then our **responsibilities** are sacred.

Locke believed that free societies survive only when individuals possess internal restraint—what he called *reason guided by law.* Freedom without virtue, he warned, devolves into license. His philosophy laid the moral foundation for democracy, asserting that **self-government depends on self-discipline.**

For our time, Locke's message couldn't be clearer. We are surrounded by freedoms—speech, choice, identity—but we've forgotten that freedom isn't the goal; it's the **test**. Every right we claim demands an equal measure of responsibility in return.

Lesson: You can't build a meaningful life—or a stable nation—without moral boundaries. Rules don't confine freedom; they preserve it.

Jordan Peterson: Responsibility as the Path to Meaning

Where Locke anchored freedom in virtue, **Jordan Peterson** has reintroduced the concept of virtue into modern psychology. In a world obsessed with self-esteem and victimhood, Peterson reminds young people—especially men—that fulfillment is found not in comfort but in **shouldering responsibility.**

He writes in *12 Rules for Life:*

"Pick up your cross and bear it as best you can. It's the most meaningful thing you can do."

That message resonates because it fills a void. Too many young men have been told that masculinity is inherently toxic or obsolete. Peterson offers an alternative: **responsibility as redemption.** He challenges his audience to clean their rooms before they try to fix the world—not because tidiness will save humanity, but because *order begins within.*

Peterson's advice aligns closely with something I tell my boys when I explain my own definition of manhood: *A man is someone who not only takes responsibility for himself, but for others.* Simply not being a burden to others isn't enough. Authentic manhood means being the one others can depend on—physically, emotionally, and morally. It's standing tall not for pride's sake, but because others may need the strength you bring.

That principle echoes across all the thinkers in this chapter. **Peck** taught that discipline is the foundation of love. **Warren** showed that purpose grows through service. **Locke** warned that freedom dies without virtue. And **Peterson** now reminds a new generation that meaning arises only through voluntary burden.

Lesson: Responsibility is the antidote to despair. The moment you decide your actions matter, your suffering gains context—and purpose replaces chaos.

Bringing It All Together

Across generations and ideologies, these thinkers converge on a single truth: **faith, discipline, freedom, and responsibility are not competing values—they are interdependent virtues.**

Peck teaches us to grow through hardship.

Warren reminds us that purpose is discovered in service.

Locke insists that liberty requires morality.

Peterson calls us to reclaim meaning through responsibility.

For Gen X, these lessons reinforce what we've already learned through experience—that maturity and faith are built, not given. For Gen Z, they offer a roadmap through the noise: truth over convenience, service over self, responsibility over resentment.

No matter where you stand on faith or philosophy, these four voices agree on one essential principle: a purposeful life is one lived **with courage, conscience, and contribution.**

In Practice

Start small. Make your bed, balance your budget, keep your word. Integrity begins with ordinary habits.

Serve something bigger. Volunteer, mentor, teach, or simply show up for someone who needs you.

Tell the truth—especially to yourself. Self-deception erodes freedom from the inside out.

Protect your freedom by practicing restraint. Rights mean little without self-control.

Carry responsibility willingly. The weight you choose defines the strength you build.

Discipline without faith hardens the heart. Faith without discipline weakens it. The synthesis of both—that's where purpose lives.

As Peck would say, *"The road less traveled"* is not the easiest path, but it's the only one that leads anywhere worth going.

If there's one truth history has proven time and again, it's that no civilization collapses from the outside first—it collapses from within. Empires don't die because enemies become stronger; they die because people stop believing in what made them great. The same is true for individuals. When belief erodes, purpose fades. When purpose fades, freedom eventually follows.

Faith—whether in God, principle, or something greater than self—has always been the invisible scaffolding that holds a nation together. It is what turns liberty from license into stewardship. **John Locke** understood this when he wrote that all men are "the workmanship of one omnipotent and infinitely wise Maker." To him, faith wasn't just a private conviction; it was the foundation of justice itself. Rights that come from God can't be taken by kings, mobs, or governments. But Locke also warned that freedom cannot survive without virtue, without citizens capable of governing themselves before governing others.

That principle has echoed through every generation of American life, and it's being tested again today. We've mistaken abundance for strength, and opinion for truth. We've learned to speak freely but forgotten how to communicate responsibly. As the walls of faith have weakened, so has our sense of shared purpose. **Freedom without moral conviction becomes chaos. Faith without moral courage becomes hypocrisy.** Our challenge is to restore both—within ourselves first, and then within our culture.

The **moral survival of nations** depends on ordinary people living extraordinary principles. It doesn't begin in the Capitol or the courthouse—it starts at the dinner table, in the classroom, and in the quiet moments when we decide whether to tell the truth, keep our word, or forgive an enemy. Those are the decisions that hold civilizations together.

As **Scott Peck** taught, "Love is the will to extend oneself for the purpose of nurturing one's own or another's spiritual growth." Nations grow the same way—through the will to extend ourselves beyond comfort for the good of others.

Rick Warren reminded us that "It's not about you." That's not a denial of individuality—it's a call to service. We are at our best, both as people and as a people, when we live for something larger than ourselves.

Jordan Peterson reframed that service for a modern world drowning in cynicism. His challenge to "pick up your cross and bear it" is not just religious—it's practical. It's a blueprint for meaning in an age of confusion. As he tells his students, "Stand up straight with your shoulders back"—not because posture solves everything, but because *posture precedes purpose.*

And **Locke's** wisdom reminds us that freedom is not our birthright—it's our inheritance. Like all inheritances, it can be squandered if not renewed.

That renewal begins with us. Every generation must choose whether to live as consumers of freedom or as stewards of it. Faith is what gives that stewardship endurance. It's the unseen force that ties our private morality to our public responsibility.

For **Gen X**, our role is to bridge the divide—to show through our example that faith and reason, individuality and duty, can coexist. For **Gen Z**, the call is to take the authenticity you value so deeply and anchor it to something enduring. You are not adrift in chaos; you are standing at the same crossroads every generation before you has faced—the choice between living for comfort or living for purpose.

True freedom doesn't come from doing whatever you want; it comes from doing what you *ought*. It comes from living by principle even when it costs you something. That's what gives freedom its strength—when people choose right over easy, service over self, and meaning over pleasure.

Faith is what makes that choice possible. It's what turns conviction into courage. It's what allows us to walk forward even when we can't see the whole road ahead.

So wherever you stand on belief—Christian, skeptic, or something in between—remember this: freedom survives only when people are willing to carry its weight. That weight is moral, not political. It's personal before it's public.

And when we each carry that small share of responsibility, something miraculous happens. Families heal. Communities strengthen. Nations endure.

Because in the end, **faith is not about knowing—it's about choosing.** It's the decision to live as though your life has purpose, your freedom has meaning, and your actions matter.

That's the quiet revolution this generation must lead—not through outrage, but through example. Not by tearing down what came before, but by rebuilding what was lost: **discipline, humility, and service.**

As I tell my sons: *The measure of a man—or a nation—is not how much power he holds, but how much responsibility he carries.*

So carry it.

Not because it's easy.

Not because it's glamorous.

But because it's right.

Faith and freedom are living things—they thrive only when we choose to nurture them.

A Final Thought…

In the end, the story of faith and freedom is the story of renewal—of one generation passing to the next, not just opportunity, but moral responsibility as well. Gen Z now stands where every "next greatest generation" begins: at the point where comfort must give way to conviction. Their strength won't come from inherited wealth, technology, or power—it will come from rediscovering what makes freedom worth preserving. If they can ground their authenticity in moral purpose, their passion in discipline, and their independence in faith, they won't just inherit a nation—they'll redefine it. Because the true test of greatness isn't what a generation receives, but what it chooses to believe in, stand for, and pass forward.

---

[1] Barna Group. *Belief in Jesus Rises Among Gen Z and Millennials.* Barna Research, 2025. Available at: https://www.barna.com/research/belief-in-jesus-rises/

[2] Barna Group. *Young Adults Lead a Resurgence in Church Attendance.* Barna Research, 2025. Available at: https://www.barna.com/research/young-adults-lead-resurgence-in-church-attendance/

[3] Axios. "Religious Young People Are Fueling a Christian Resurgence." *Axios*, May 10, 2025. Available at: https://www.axios.com/2025/05/10/religious-young-people-christianity-rise

[4] Axios. "Gen Z Men Are More Religious Than Gen Z Women, Poll Shows." *Axios*, Sept 28, 2024. Available at: https://www.axios.com/2024/09/28/religion-poll-gen-z-men-women-gap

[5] The Washington Post. "Jordan Peterson Is on a Crusade to Toughen Up Young Men. It's Landed Him on Our Cultural Divide." *The Washington Post*, May 2, 2018. Available at: https://www.washingtonpost.com/lifestyle/style/jordan-peterson-is-on-a-crusade-to-toughen-up-young-men-its-

landed-him-on-our-cultural-divide/2018/05/02/c5bafe48-31d6-11e8-94fa-32d48460b955_story.html

[6] The Daily Signal. "I Found Young Men—and They're Listening: Why Jordan Peterson Matters." *The Daily Signal*, June 13, 2024. Available at: https://www.dailysignal.com/2024/06/13/i-found-young-men-theyre-listening-jordan-peterson/

[7] American Philosophical Association Blog. "Why Are So Many Young Men Drawn to Jordan Peterson's Intellectual Misogyny?" *APA Blog*, Feb 20, 2018. Available at: https://blog.apaonline.org/2018/02/20/why-are-so-many-young-men-drawn-to-jordan-petersons-intellectual-misogyny/

Epilogue: A Letter to the Next Greatest Generation

To the young men and women who will inherit what we've built — and what we've broken — this is my final message.

The world you're stepping into is louder, faster, and more uncertain than the one I grew up in. You'll be told that everything is relative, that truth is subjective, and that strength is outdated. But don't believe it. The noise will fade. What lasts are the quiet things — integrity, discipline, faith, and love.

Every generation before you has faced its own test. Some passed, some failed, and some merely survived. The "Greatest Generation" earned that name not because of their circumstances, but because of their character. They rose to meet impossible odds with humility and courage. They didn't wait for ideal conditions or perfect leaders; they became the people their time required.

You will have your own version of that test. It may not look like war or depression, but it will require the same strength of spirit — the ability to stand firm when everything around you trembles, to lead when others hesitate, and to choose what's right when it costs you something.

If my generation has anything to offer, it's perspective. We've seen comfort become captivity, distraction become dependence, and cynicism replace hope. But we've also seen what happens when people decide that enough is enough — when they return to truth, rebuild families, and rediscover purpose.

You don't need to save the world overnight. You just need to begin by saving the space around you — your home, your friendships, your community. Great movements are never born in stadiums or hashtags; they begin in the quiet decisions of individuals who choose principle over popularity.

You will be tempted to measure your worth in likes, followers, or titles. But the real measure of a life is whether people are better because you lived it. Did you leave the world a little more honest? Did you help someone stand who would've fallen? Did you love even when it wasn't returned? Those are the questions that define greatness.

Remember, too, that freedom isn't self-sustaining. It depends on the character of its citizens — on people willing to do hard things without applause. If faith is the foundation of freedom, then discipline is the frame that holds it upright. Lose either, and the whole structure collapses.

I don't expect you to agree with everything in this book. My generation didn't always get it right, and neither will yours. But if you can take these lessons — the stories, the scars, and the truths we learned the hard way — and make something better from them, then we will have succeeded.

The baton is in your hands now. What you do with it will shape not just your future, but the moral future of this nation. You were not made for comfort; you were made for purpose. Don't let fear or cynicism convince you otherwise.

When the day comes that you're the one giving advice — to your children or to the next generation after you — I hope you can say you stood firm when it mattered, that you lived with conviction, and that you helped rebuild a world worth inheriting.

If you do that, you won't just be part of the next generation.
You'll be part of the **next greatest generation.**

— *A Gen X Dad*

About the Author

Dr. Jeff Hogan is a retired U.S. Air Force Lieutenant Colonel, defense contractor, and writer whose work explores the intersection of faith, freedom, and generational responsibility. A proud member of Generation X, he brings to his writing the hard-earned lessons of service, leadership, and fatherhood — lessons born from decades spent navigating both warfighting and peace, the analog world of his youth, and the digital age that followed.

Commissioned in June 1990, Jeff served on active duty from December 1990 to June 2001 before continuing his career as an Individual Mobilization Augmentee (IMA) until his retirement in July 2018. Over the course of nearly three decades in uniform, he witnessed firsthand how discipline, sacrifice, and purpose shape not only missions, but lives.

After leaving active duty, Jeff began a defense contracting career that has spanned more than two decades, working for industry leaders including **Aerojet, Northrop Grumman, Lockheed Martin, Orbital Sciences,** and **USfalcon.** His professional journey has centered on advancing space and defense programs while mentoring the next generation of professionals entering national service.

Jeff holds a **Bachelor of Science in Physics** from *San José State University*, a **Master of Arts in Space Systems Management** from *Webster University*, and a **Doctor of Philosophy in Professional Studies in Education** from *Capella University.*

Beyond his career, Jeff is a husband, father, and lifelong learner. He enjoys traveling with his wife, **Kamma**, hiking, snorkeling, camping, aquaponic gardening, coaching athletes for **Special Olympics**, and — most recently — gold panning in the mountains of Colorado. He currently resides in **Parker, Colorado**, and looks forward to retiring someday on a quiet beach along the **Mexican Riviera.**

The Next Greatest Generation is his first major published work, written as both a message to his three sons — **Julian, Quinn, and Ian** — and a call to all young men and women to rediscover the timeless virtues that sustain freedom, faith, and purpose across generations.

Acknowledgements

No book is ever written alone. Every idea in these pages was shaped by the people who challenged, encouraged, and inspired me along the way.

First and foremost, I owe everything to my wife, **Kamma**, whose belief and faith in me kept me grounded when life pulled in every other direction. To my sons — **Julian, Quinn, and Ian** — you are the reason this book exists. You've each taught me that the lessons we try to pass down are only as real as the lives that receive them. Watching you grow into men of purpose has been my greatest honor.

I'm grateful to the friends, mentors, and colleagues who helped me sharpen the ideas within these chapters — the people who weren't afraid to ask hard questions or point out when I'd drifted off course. Their feedback reminded me that honest conversation is still the most powerful teacher.

To my editors, early readers, and fellow veterans who offered both technical and moral guidance: thank you for your time, precision, and belief that the message mattered.

In keeping with the spirit of this book — where wisdom meets innovation — I used **AI-assisted tools** to help research, structure, and refine the manuscript. These tools did not create the message; they simply helped illuminate it.

Finally, thank you to every reader who chooses to wrestle with these pages instead of scrolling past them. The future belongs to those willing to think, to question, and to build. If anything, here strengthens your faith, your discipline, or your hope in what's possible, then this effort has done its job.

— *Jeff Hogan*

www.ingramcontent.com/pod-product-compliance
Lightning Source LLC
LaVergne TN
LVHW010654110826
845149LV00014B/3079

* 9 7 8 1 9 6 6 6 2 5 9 7 1 *